DON'T BE STOIC

Ancient Wisdom for Troubled Times

Peter J. Vernezze

University Press of America,® Inc.
Lanham · Boulder · New York · Toronto · Oxford

Copyright © 2005 by
University Press of America,® Inc.
4501 Forbes Boulevard
Suite 200
Lanham, Maryland 20706
UPA Acquisitions Department (301) 459-3366

PO Box 317
Oxford
OX2 9RU, UK

All rights reserved
Printed in the United States of America
British Library Cataloging in Publication Information Available

Library of Congress Control Number: 2004111814
ISBN 0-7618-3014-6 (paperback : alk. ppr.)

To the memory of my sister, Patricia Mercier-Gross

Contents

Preface	vii
Introduction: Stoicism: The Path to Personal Liberation	xi
Chapter One: Difficulties and Disappointments	1

The Stoic with a Porsche
One Step to Financial Freedom
Show Me the Money
A Fool's Paradise
On a Run
Stoics in Love
The Last Day of the Rest of Your Life
Suicide and Stoicism
The Golden Years
In Sickness and in Health

Chapter Two: Destructive Emotions	33

Little Things
Edith Piaf, Stoic
Fear and Loathing in Stoicism
Keeping Company with the Abyss
Stoic Grief
Emotionally Intelligent Stoics
Don't Worry, Be Stoic
Tragic Optimism
Stoics and Society
Are Stoics Happy?
A Modern Day Stoic

Chapter Three: Miscellaneous Matters 75
The God of the Stoics
When Bad Things Happen to Good Stoics
Was the Buddha a Stoic?
Satori and Stoicism
Tuesdays with Marcus
Practice, Practice, Practice
Do I Contradict Myself?
Be Prepared
Three Years

Notes 113

Index 119

Preface

What follows is a collection of essays inspired by Stoic thought. Although Stoic philosophy comprises physics, logic, and ethics, I have focused on the ethical components of Stoic thought in general and in particular on the writings of three men from a relatively late period in the development of Stoicism. Perhaps the most famous (and most unlikely) Stoic is the Roman emperor Marcus Aurelius (121-180 A.D.), who by all accounts consistently managed to integrate the severe dictates of Stoic ethics into a life of privilege and power. His *Meditations*, a collection of brief reflections, quotes, and comments on the human condition, is probably the most well-known and certainly well-loved Stoic text.

Epictetus (55-135 A.D.) traces his origins from the other end of the social spectrum. Born a Greek slave, Epictetus was freed at age eighteen and spent most of his life as a teacher. Although we possess nothing from his own hand, his words were recorded by his pupil, Arrian, in four books of *Discourses* and in a short summary of Epictetus' thought that we know as the *Handbook*. Among the most prolific of the Stoics, Seneca (4 B.C.-65 A.D.) was not only a philosopher but a playwright and statesman whose career paralleled the ups and downs of many in the Roman empire. Exiled in 41 A.D., Seneca was recalled some eight years later to be tutor to the young Nero, fell into and out of favor with the emperor, and was ultimately required to commit suicide. His letters to Lucilius and his numerous moral essays provide insight into a man struggling, not always successfully, to live up to his high ideals.

This is a very unusual work and it has had the support of some very unusual people. Friends and colleagues at too numerous to name have read sections of the work, commented on its central ideas, and sometimes assisted simply by serving as living illustrations of the power of Stoic doctrine. I would especially like to acknowledge my departed and much revered fellow philosopher Jennings Olsen, who served as a mentor and an example of Stoicism in action. I would like to thank Weber State University for a one semester sabbatical to study the connections between Buddhism and Stoicism at Naropa University in Boulder, Colorado. Dr. Albert Ellis provided inspiration both through his work and through some kind words of encouragement in correspondence early on in this project. I have always kept a copy of his *A Guide to Rational Living* besides *The Meditations* of Marcus Aurelius. Deborah Peterson painstakingly edited the essays section of this work. Warren Pettey assisted in the final proofreading. Any errors, however, are my own. This project could not have been completed without the support of my parents, Francis and DeLoris Vernezze, and my sister Mary. My greatest debt, however, is to Pamela Hall, the muse behind everything I do.

Acknowledgments

All excerpts from Epictetus reprinted by permission of the publishers and Trustees of the Loeb Classical Library from EPICTETUS: VOLUMES I & II, Loeb Classical Library® Volume L 131 and Volume L 218, translated by W.A. Oldfather, Cambridge, Mass: Harvard University Press, 1925 & 1928. The Loeb Classical Library® is a registered trademark of the President and Fellows of Harvard College.

Stoicism: The Path to Personal Liberation

You can be happy right now—regardless of your circumstances. You don't have to lose weight, have money to invest in the stock market, or accept Jesus as your personal savior. What is required, instead, is one simple insight and the knowledge of how to apply this insight to your life.

Sound easy? Well it's not. The insight is one we don't particularly want to hear, and the ability to integrate it into our lives will require patience, effort, and discipline. But if you're willing to listen to some unpleasant truths and courageous enough to act upon them, the system I am about to introduce can not only be of assistance in getting you through whatever personal challenges you are currently facing, but it can also serve as a road map to a healthier view of reality and a guide to a more satisfying life.

But you don't have to take my word for it. Stoicism has been around for over two thousand years, assisting men and women from all walks of life in confronting personal loss, financial uncertainty, societal upheaval, anxiety, sickness, and death—the whole panoply of ills that afflict us. And Stoicism rarely disappoints, providing solace, consolation, perspective, and most importantly, wisdom, for generations upon generations of people who have turned to it in troubling times. This is doubtless the reason that one Stoic classic, the *Meditations* of Marcus Aurelius, remains on bookstore shelves some two thousand years after it was first written. But though one often stumbles into Stoicism as a

xii   Introduction

result of personal difficulties, just as regularly one stays with the system
long after the troubles have subsided. In the same way that it might take
an illness to finally generate a proper concern for health, so also can the
bad times which often bring us to Stoicism can lay the foundation for a
return to balance, perspective, and sanity in our lives.

Stoicism: What is it?

Ask for a definition of the word "Stoic" and you might get the following: A "Stoic" is someone who bears up well under great difficulty. The
respondent might even illustrate this point with a story about an uncle
or distant cousin who, faced with a terminal illness, complained little
and even managed to cheer up others. Although there is nothing wrong
with such a reply, neither is it particularly enlightening. It would be as
if the word "Christian" had lost all of its other connotations and had
simply come to mean "turning the other cheek." True enough, we might
say, though in fact this is merely one of the doctrines of Christianity,
and tells us nothing about the wisdom of the man who uttered it or the
grandeur of the system that embodied it. Similarly, behind the innocent
term "Stoic" is a philosophical system whose scope and influence it is
hard for us to comprehend.

For nearly five centuries, Stoicism reigned as the predominant
philosophy of the West. Yet it survives today mainly through a few
original texts, a legacy of historical influence on Christian ethics, and
an occasional literary portrayal, as in Tom Wolfe's recent novel, *A Man
in Full*. For a significant number of people, however, Stoicism remains
much more than a historical footnote. This group, which consists
mainly of spiritually active individuals who find themselves alienated
from traditional Western religion, discover in Stoicism a system with
neither a Judeo-Christian God nor a doctrine of an afterlife, but a
system which nevertheless provides profound moral and spiritual
guidance. This might seem surprising, for we have been led to believe
that without a Deity or the threat of retribution morality degenerates
into dangerous relativism, and life likewise sinks into a meaningless
jumble. The two thousand year tradition of Stoicism proves such a
simplification sadly mistaken.

It is my goal in this essay to offer a glimpse into a philosophy whose
long term survival testifies to its standing as one of the wisdom systems
of the world. Just like a biography will often commence by reviewing
the subject's genealogy, so perhaps the best place to begin an examina-

Stoicism: The Path to Personal Liberation

tion of Stoicism is with a study of the intellectual soil from which it sprang. Morality in the West can properly be said to start with the Homeric epics, *Iliad* and *Odyssey*. These works laid out a code of behavior for generations of Greeks, a code embodied in the lives of the heroes Agamemnon, Achilles, Hector, Ajax, and Odysseus. To most people today, these names mean nothing. But to the ancient Greeks, these individuals served as models of conduct in the same way as John Wayne once did for a generation of Americans. Their strength and courage, as well as their wealth, noble birth, and physical beauty, provided the ideals to be imitated by those in search of ethical excellence. However this warrior code, which primarily valued characteristics required for success in battle, was not without its problems. It tended to be egoistic, requiring each individual to emphasize his own interest, sometimes at the expense of the overall good. This could result in otherwise heroic figures appearing rather petty, as when Achilles withdraws from battle because Agamemnon deprives him of a favorite slave girl in retribution for his insolence. This system of ethics also excluded large segments of the population, women in particular, from any moral consideration. But perhaps the most significant characteristic of the warrior code for our purposes was that it located the standard by which an individual was to be judged good or bad outside of the individual. For those living with this Homeric outlook, goodness depended upon the ability to live up to the ideal of the warrior.

In very different ways Plato and Aristotle, who represent the next significant development in the history of ethics, incorporate this notion of placing the ultimate ethical judgment in an external source. For Plato, ethical standards arise not out of a societal construction but are a part of the fabric of reality. A transcendent realm of eternal entities is responsible for the objects of this world having the characteristics that they do. This metaphysical scheme, known as Plato's Theory of Forms or Ideas, has been subject to debate, hostility, and misinterpretation since it was first proposed. But its spirit still lingers. The beautiful objects of this world fade and pass away, but the Form of Beauty remains: eternal, uncreated, and unchanging, a standard against which all beautiful objects are measured (and invariably fall short). Ethical ideals follow the same pattern. Good does not depend upon human judgments, which are variable and subject to change. Rather, good resides in this eternal realm, thus allowing the possibility of absolute ethical judgments for perhaps the first time in Western history. As ennobling as such a theory is, and as odd and otherworldly as it must have sounded to Plato's contemporaries, this value scheme shares with the warrior code the characteristic of holding humans accountable to an external ideal. Both ethical systems look outward for answers: the warrior code to the concept of the hero, Plato to the eternal Forms.

Opposing his teacher on every conceivable topic, Aristotle took issue with the Platonic value scheme as well. Rather than find ethical truth in another world, Aristotle is convinced that the only good is a human one. Hence, good is to be understood in terms of traits that an individual human being could embody. By bringing ethics down to earth and eliminating as superfluous the notion of a separately existing standard, however, Aristotle returns to a sense of right and wrong that shares important similarities with the Homeric code. To be sure, Aristotle greatly refines the Homeric ideal, adding virtues such as temperance and generosity to the catalog of traits an individual should possess. In addition, Aristotle's good man famously seeks moderation in all things, an idea obviously foreign to warriors such as Achilles. Like the earlier conception, however, Aristotle's good man exhibits many characteristics of the aristocratic Athenian of his day. Although Aristotle's ideal is less war-like than the Homeric, the underlying ethical rationale sounds strikingly familiar, for what is good is measured by a societal standard.

It is on this historical stage that Stoicism makes its appearance. Zeno, the legendary founder of the system, begins lecturing in Athens a couple of decades after Aristotle's death. His system will change the history of ethics in the same way that certain earthquakes can reverse the course of rivers. At the heart of his divergence from his predecessors is what I will refer to as the Inward Turn. For all of their differences, the Homeric, Platonic, and Aristotelian systems are alike in that they locate the standard of ultimate judgment and the source of behavioral guidelines outside of the individual. For Homer, it is the warrior; for Aristotle, the aristocrat; for Plato, the eternal and unchanging Form. With Stoicism, as we will see, the situation becomes radically altered.

The Swiss psychologist C.G. Jung speculated that at a certain period of life, usually around the time of Dante's "halfway through life's journey," individuals must seriously undertake a process of introversion, looking into themselves rather than at the world for answers. This will involve examining the extent to which goals have been the product not of inner callings but of parental demands, societal pressures, and random choices. By pulling away from extraneous influences and learning to listen to our inner urges, priorities will often alter and life changes occur. Indeed, Jung goes further and claims that without such

Stoicism: The Path to Personal Liberation

xv

severe self-scrutiny, maturation is not possible.

Stoicism, I believe, represents a similar stage in the history of ethics—a rejection of external standards of judgment and a search for a code of behavior that has its source in the self. Interestingly, Stoicism begins this radical divergence with an assumption that would not have seemed at all peculiar to its predecessors. Like all of early Greek ethics, Stoicism takes as its starting point the notion that happiness is the ultimate goal of life. Dubbed eudaimonism (after "eudaimonia," the Greek word for happiness), this thesis will be rejected by Christianity and replaced with the view that our purpose in this life is to develop ourselves for the next. But in classical Greek times, the next world, to the extent that it is conceived of at all, is invariably thought of as a dismal region of darkness. So the focus on achieving happiness here and now is natural enough. (Indeed, if we are to believe Nietzsche, it is precisely their inability to achieve happiness in this life that causes early Christians to posit a next).

What, then, is happiness, and how are we to achieve it? Answers to this question have certainly not been lacking in the history of Western thought. The Stoic view, to put it somewhat crudely, is that we are happy when we are able to satisfy our desires (and unhappy when we are not able to fulfill them). "Happiness must already possess everything that it wants,"[1] says Epictetus. With this statement, Stoicism reveals another of its radical characteristics, for Stoicism is the great democratizer of ethics. The Homeric, Platonic, and Aristotelian views are elitist, asserting that the good life is available only for a select few—those with either strength, intelligence, or aristocratic upbringing. But since everyone has desires, Stoicism places no theoretical constraints on who may achieve the human good. Perhaps for the first time in Western thought, happiness is available to everybody!

But if Stoicism seems in principle to make happiness available to all, from another perspective it can be accused of denying it to everyone as well. For who can satisfy all of her desires? Most of us do not possess the means to undertake this daunting task. And even the billionaire must run up against obstacles in the form of things she cannot own and people she cannot buy. Furthermore, her desire not to get sick, grow old, or die will inevitably be thwarted. Happiness, it seems, is unattainable. Unless . . . .

Unless, say the Stoics, we take a radically different attitude. Here it is time to discuss the insight alluded to at the start of this essay. It was stated in its purest form by the Stoic philosopher Epictetus in the first

xvi Introduction

century A.D. It comes in two parts and begins as follows:

> Some things are under our control, while others are not. Under our control are conception, choice, desire, aversion, and, in a word, everything that is our own doing; not under our control our are body, our property, reputation, office, and, in a word, everything that is not our own doing.[2]

The insight, then, informs us that there is a distinction between what we can and cannot control. Now at one level this is hardly news. We know, for example, that we can't control the weather, but we believe that we are perfectly capable of stopping ourselves from shooting a belligerent neighbor. But once we get past these basics, we run into all sorts of difficulties over where to draw the line. Indeed, if Stoics are right, we live as if whole parts of our lives are within our control which in fact are not. For example, I find myself getting angry because I am stuck in traffic and late for an appointment. Here, I neglect the one thing I can control—my emotional reaction—and focus energy on the congestion, a state of affairs over which I have no say whatsoever.

But the results of mistaking what I can and cannot control reach much further than traffic jams. Tom works for a dot.com start up. In the course of a few years, he's purchased a beautiful home, a new car, and all the gadgets he's ever wanted; he has accumulated quite an impressive nest egg; he has a beautiful wife and a bright future. But the market crashes, his business goes under, and suddenly all that is taken away. One by one the possessions are sold; the retirement account, which consisted of company stock, is completely wiped out; and his wife, who envisioned things quite differently, leaves him. Tom is devastated and Stoics are not surprised. What else is to be expected from identifying our well-being with states of affairs we cannot ultimately control?

Although this is an extreme case, it makes an important point. We accumulate houses, cars, stereos, and personal computers; we research and invest in order to build a portfolio; we devote ourselves almost religiously to our jobs; we work out, eat right, and perhaps even undergo expensive surgery in order to maintain our bodily appearance. We do all this in the belief that these things have some sort of permanence, as if there existed a reasonable certainty that we could maintain our property, job, money, and health indefinitely and count on these as the source of our future happiness. But the fact is, as Tom found out and as many of us discover as well, that it can all be taken away (and

Stoicism: The Path to Personal Liberation   xvii

eventually with the passage of time will be taken away). In stark contrast to these externals over which we have no ultimate control, there is one thing which we can never voluntarily be deprived of: our ability to react to any situation with equanimity.

Up until this point, we have been dealing with the merely factual part of the insight. The Stoics have provided us with a piece of information, namely, that there exists a difference between what we can and cannot control. They have also argued that no more and no less than one thing in the entire universe falls into the latter category, for we can only ultimately control how we react to a given situation. But there is an evaluative component to all this as well. That is, the two categories—what we can and cannot control—are not merely logically distinct but in fact represent qualitatively different realms:

> The things that are under our control are by nature free, unhindered and unimpeded; while the things that are not under our control are weak, servile, subject to hindrance, and not our own. Remember, therefore, that if what is naturally slavish you think to be free, and what is not your own to be your own, you will be hampered, will grieve, will be in turmoil, and will blame both god and men; while if you think only what is your own to be your own...then no one will ever be able to exert compulsion upon you, no one will hinder you, you will blame no one, will find fault with no one, [and] no one will harm you.[3]

In short, the things we can control are more valuable that those we cannot, since the former contain the key to our freedom and happiness. Here, we recognize the echo of an age-old wisdom. Fairy tales speak of the discarded object in fact being the treasure; the Bible relates how the stone that the builders reject becomes the cornerstone. The Stoics similarly inform us that a great power lies at our feet, unrecognized by us, and we refuse to take it up. We focus our energy and effort on things that are ultimately beyond our control—job, health, material possessions, et cetera. But in so doing, Stoics tell us that we are bound to be upset, anxious, and discontented, since circumstances can always overturn these perceived certainties. Fred is an aspiring writer whose manuscripts keep getting rejected; Susan has planned her whole life around becoming a doctor only to fail to get into medical school; Margaret sits seething because her friends have nicer homes, smarter children, and better vacations; Frank finds himself passed over time and again for promotion.

xviii   Introduction

In these and similar cases, individuals place their happiness, self-worth, and even their sanity in things over which they have no ultimate control. This, the insight informs us, is precisely the wrong path. Instead of focusing on what we cannot control, we need to direct our energy towards the one thing that is truly up to us. A permanent and unshakable source of strength lies within our grasp that nothing can undermine, since we can always and everywhere control how we react in a given situation. "It is always in your power to live in the greatest tranquility of mind."[4] That is, it is possible to view otherwise unpleasant situations with grace and gratitude, to see difficulties as a source of strength rather than a severe setback, and to gain wisdom and understanding from the inevitable. In short, we can choose to react with calmness, contentment, and tranquility rather than frustration, anger, and anxiety. This simple yet invulnerable power holds the key to our happiness.

Critiques and Criticisms

Epictetus assures his students that following his system will bring them "tranquility and freedom from emotional perturbation."[5] The Roman emperor and Stoic philosopher Marcus Aurelius asserts that it is possible to "live a life which flows quietly, and is like the existence of the gods,"[6] while Seneca declares that the Stoic's mind can "abide in serenity without excitement or depression."[7] Upon hearing a description of the Stoic ideal, people generally have one of two diametrically opposed reactions. Some raise serious questions about the psychological feasibility of the Stoic endeavor. As pleasant as the prospect of an unperturbed existence sounds, life, this group asserts, is simply too stressful and chaotic to walk through it in the constant state of tranquility that the Stoics describe. Others view the Stoic goal as attainable but unattractive. According to these dissenters, to go through one's days in the controlled and even-keeled manner that the Stoics depict would be to miss the ups and downs, the agony and the ecstasy, that make life worth living.

To the first group, Stoics insist that the life of tranquility and contentment they describe is indeed within our grasp, although they admit that reaching this goal is far from easy. You don't simply turn on a bliss switch and have all your problems go away. "Nothing is done except for a price,"[8] Epictetus reminds us. We will have to reexamine our lives, revise our priorities, and establish a different relationship both with ourselves and with the world, all the while engaging in a constant watchfulness over the contents of our minds. Epictetus presents the analogy of an athlete in training for an Olympic contest as the proper analogy for the sort of effort he is advocating.[9] As in the case of the athlete, success will come only with a good deal of effort and not an insignificant amount of time. "A bull is not made suddenly, nor a brave man. We must first discipline ourselves for a winter campaign."[10]

The response to those who bring forth the second charge is a bit more complex, for Stoics admit the truth of part of their accusation by denying any value to the sort of bouncing back and forth between emotional extremes that the objectors depict as their preferred condition. Instead of getting tremendously excited or upset at most of the events that come our way, the Stoic seeks to confront the days in tranquility and freedom from disturbance. The strategy is roughly akin to the one used in this oft-repeated story. A man wins a beautiful horse. His neighbors extol his good fortune, but the man is skeptical. "Good. Bad. Who can tell?" he says. Shortly thereafter, the man's son is crippled in a fall from the horse. His neighbors rush to console him, but he simply replies, "Good. Bad. Who can tell?" His response seems confirmed when the army rides through seeking recruits. Because his son is injured, they refuse to take him. One day the horse runs away. By now the neighbors are getting the point. They say nothing, and so are not surprised when the horse returns a few days later followed by a dozen more horses. Rather than being thrown into ecstasy at one moment and plunged into despair the next, the Stoic possesses a sense of perspective and a realization that most of the things that upset and delight us are simply not worth getting that worked up about. As Seneca puts it: "Never have I trusted fortune, even when she seemed to be at peace; all her generous bounties–money, office, influence—I deposited where she could ask for them back without disturbing me."[11]

But the refusal to go to emotional extremes does not mean that Stoics are unfeeling, emotionless automata. This, they insist, is a false dichotomy. Indeed, Stoics describe their own emotional ideal in very different words than the dour terms that their critics imagine. Epictetus emphasizes the true Stoic state of mind when he declares that his system will allow one to live "with a light heart and an obedient disposition; with a gentle spirit awaiting anything that may befall and enduring that which has already befallen."[12] Marcus exhorts us to "be cheerful,"[13] while Seneca encourages a correspondent to "learn how to feel joy."[14]

How could their critics have gone so wrong in their assessment of the emotional life of the Stoic? If joy is not a term usually associated with Stoicism, this is because of the mistaken belief that only someone who is effusively spewing out his emotions can be joyful. This represents, at best, a greatly simplified understanding of joy. Seneca tries to correct this impression in one of his letters, claiming that there are, in fact, two different joys: the state that passes for joy in most people and the joy that Stoics experience. Dependent upon circumstances and disappearing as quickly as it arises, the joy felt by the masses is "but a thin pleasure."[15] By contrast, Stoic joy is the product of a sustained effort and lasts a lifetime. Since the Stoic knows he can remain unperturbed in all circumstances, he exists fully in the present moment: content with his lot, desiring nothing but what the days bring, grateful towards the gods, and well-disposed towards humanity. If this is not joy (and if it is not, what is?), it at least seems as far from emotional deadness as I can imagine.

Stoicism Today

In the following pages I demonstrate how to utilize Stoic wisdom in order to transform our troubles and deal effectively with disappointment, difficulty, and destructive emotions. Now this is not, as I pointed out at the beginning, a pleasant thing to hear. Stoicism asks us not to avert our eyes from the darker side of life, but the truth is that we Americans don't like to be reminded about such things. We like success stories; we demand happy endings; we buy books that tell us how we can have it all: be spiritually fulfilled, physically fit, financially successful, and sexually satisfied.

But the high expectations imposed by this "cult of optimism" can have damaging and devastating consequences. Invariably, those who fail to live up to this unrealistic standard become the modern day lepers. The elderly are perhaps the most numerous component of this group. We avoid the old and shuttle them off to nursing homes so that we don't have to deal with our own impending mortality. And who wants to be reminded of an acquaintance with cancer, or one who is unemployed, or suffering from mental illness, or living with chronic pain, or going through an ugly divorce, or dealing with the death of a child? Finally, there is the fact that our own lives can't help but fail to match the glittering images proposed as ideals on television and in the movies.

Our lives can fall apart in a number of ways, big and little, and

Stoicism: The Path to Personal Liberation

when they do the American dream machine is not a lot of help. By instructing us in the art of how to handle pain and loss, Stoicism serves as a necessary counterbalance to the one-sidedness of the American psyche. And even if we are fortunate enough not to currently be experiencing any major setbacks in our lives, there exists certain inevitabilities, not the least of which are old age, sickness, and death, as Buddhism reminds us. Although we would rather not contemplate these unpleasantries either, denial does not make them go away. Stoicism can provide a perspective that allows us to integrate these into our lives with insight. Finally, Stoicism thankfully can come into play in much more mundane circumstances. The thousand and one ways in which our days do not go as planned are as much a reality as anything: bad neighbors, broken down cars, credit card debt, rude waitresses, and airport delays. I could go on. And on and on. Stoicism, as you will see, can make the difference between being swamped by the wave of circumstances or riding it to a very different place.

Unexpected tragedy and loss, the inevitabilities of human existence, daily inconveniences and frustration: these are things that seem to interfere with the image of ourselves as invulnerable and destined for nothing but greatness. But life contains both darkness and light; we cannot just let in one side and be complete. Stoicism provides the framework by which we can integrate all of reality into our existence.

But it is not just for the purpose of mere survival in the face of the unpleasant aspects of life that one studies Stoicism. In reality, it is that a wisdom arises from dealing with these darker elements of our lives, as the literature of the ages demonstrates. In the Greek tragedy *Philoctetes,* the title character, a member of the Greek expedition to Troy, is seriously injured, removed from the ranks, and exiled to an island. It is revealed, however, that the gods have decreed that victory cannot be won without him. The message is clear. Just as the Greeks must take the pariah into their ranks in order to attain victory, so we must come to terms with these darker elements of our nature in order to truly triumph. A more familiar classic, the Book of Job, teaches this same lesson. The title character, having had countless sufferings unjustly visited upon him, struggles to come to terms with the question of why he, a righteous man, is being punished. Despite the ridicule of friends and the silence of God, Job is revealed at the end of the story to be a man broken on the outside but one who, as a result of his suffering, is possessed of an insight that his friends could neither attain nor appreciate.

It is in this light, finally, that I think we should view Stoicism, along xxii Introduction

the lines of that wonderful metaphor given us by Joseph Campbell: the hero's journey. In his book *The Hero with a Thousand Faces*, Campbell relates a tale that he discovers in all cultures at all times. It is the story of an individual who is pulled away from the world of everyday life, undergoes a series of experiences and adventures as a result of which he is instructed into a higher wisdom, and who, equipped with this new knowledge, returns to aid his society. It is a motif that George Lucas admits he copied when writing *Star Wars*. It is also a journey to wholeness that we all can undergo if we are willing to extricate ourselves from the illusions of eternal youth and easy wealth so pervasive in the media today and confront a radically different version of life, one that acknowledges despair and sickness, frustration and failure, loss and tragedy. To be sure, this is not easy. But in facing this reality we emerge as mature human beings who can share this perspective with a society desperately in need of it. Prior to the journey, we turned to movie stars, athletes, and business tycoons for guidance. Afterwards, we come to see that those who have suffered have much more to teach us about life. Previously, we focused on our accomplishments and joys. We now come to see that our failures, shortcomings, losses, and disappointments are equally as important and necessary. This, ultimately, is what Stoicism teaches us: the art of being human.

About the Book

The first set of essays, DIFFICULTIES AND DISAPPOINTMENTS, discusses how Stoicism can be used to grapple with the obvious problems we run up against in the *external world*, especially our relation with our own bodies, material goods, and other people. We begin with our bodies. Although we desire nothing less than health and eternal youth, as the Buddhists remind us, we are bound to be blocked in this wish and confronted instead with the reality of old age, sickness, and death. We next look outside of ourselves to the physical realm, where we likewise confront obstacles. We long for material goods and financial security only to have them elude us or fail to provide their promised bliss. Finally, much of our time in this world is spent interacting with family, friends, lovers, and an array of others. Ironically, it is precisely where we would most expect to find sympathy and fulfillment that we often discover frustration. Against this array of adversaries, the simple vision of the Stoic insight can provide a guiding light to bring one to the calm harbor of tranquility.

In the second section, DESTRUCTIVE EMOTIONS, I demonstrate how Stoicism can be applied to the disruptive *internal realm* of the passions. Frustration, regret, self-hatred, despair, and grief are all familiar companions, as are anger, anxiety, and depression. Stoicism is no stranger to any of these. But as you will see, Stoicism provides us with the mental ammunition we require to deal with these negative states, including self-awareness and a true, enduring optimism. Also, we learn that the Stoic conception of happiness, which has been the target of perennial objections, seems remarkably in line with modern psychological thought. Indeed, the whole methodology of Stoicism has parallels to a preeminent contemporary psychologist. Dr. Albert Ellis, who has been applying his own unique blend of Stoicism for forty years.

The last section of writings contains an array of information on MISCELLANEOUS MATTERS in Stoicism, including how Stoicism stacks up against traditional religion, both West and East, and some lessons in how we might go about about applying Stoicism to our daily life.

There is, of course, no substitute for reading the works of the original Stoics. But every wisdom worthy of the name must be translated anew into each generation. It is with this goal of discovering what Stoicism has to say about our current condition that I have undertaken this project. I hope you find the results useful, and that they lead you back to the source.

DIFFICULTIES AND

DISAPPOINTMENTS

The Stoic with a Porsche

The movie *A Civil Action* stars John Travolta as a personal injury lawyer who represents a small town in which the residents have had a much higher than usual incidence of death and disease due, they believe, to pollutants from companies operating near a local river. Although we see him accepting the suit primarily for mercenary reasons, during the course of the film we witness his transformation from crass opportunist into a noble crusader who is more interested in seeing justice done than in receiving any payoff. In fact, he and his firm suffer financial ruin as a result of this litigation.

The elements of the story that I find compelling are not to be found in the movie, but in the book. In the opening chapter, when the lawyer is awakened by a call informing him that his Porsche is about to be repossessed, he is unable to get a hold of his accountant and ventures outside his house—only to find sheriff's deputies have arrived to supervise the transaction. His response is, "Oh well, easy come, easy go."

It is this precise moment which is of interest–the moment in which the lawyer is transformed into a consummate Stoic. The Stoics adopted a sort of middle ground when it came to material possessions. They neither rejected external goods as inherently evil, nor did they conceive the pursuit of them to be the ultimate goal of life. Instead, they dubbed such objects "indifferents." Wealth, power, physical comfort, and even health were seen as simply irrelevant to our true well-being, as evidenced by the fact that we can be happy without them and miserable

4   Chapter One

with them. All such items were viewed as tools that could be put to good or bad use, directed towards virtuous or vicious ends. The Stoic view that material possessions have no intrinsic value is, therefore, wonderfully illustrated by the lawyer's nonchalance at the loss of his Porsche. Despite his wealth, he was not attached to the car; rather, for him it was merely a symbol of his reputation. He diverges, however, from Stoic principles in so far as he is seeking something that could also be taken away from him—his reputation. The true Stoic desires only that which he can never lose (more on this later). It may strike us as odd that a philosophy that preaches complete indifference to wealth can be perfectly embodied by someone who is basically a walking advertisement for conspicuous consumption. But it is not the things we do or do not own which make us Stoics; rather, it is our attitude towards them. We may think that the only way to demonstrate that indifference to material goods is by not possessing them, but this is a misunderstanding.

For the Stoic, the moral of the story is this: There is nothing wrong in owning expensive things, nor is there anything particularly virtuous in not owning them (though it should be said that Stoicism tends toward a level of moderation with respect to material goods). What is important is that we do not attach ourselves to our physical possessions.

Epictetus suggests the following exercise in order that we may begin to cultivate a proper attitude towards such goods. Consider something small that you own, imagine it broken and practice not being disturbed by the fact that you have lost it. "If you are fond of a jug, say, 'I am fond of a jug'; for when it is broken you will not be disturbed."[1] We need to work our way up from there, he tells us, to the big things that are invariably more difficult to let go of. Let me suggest a modern day variation on this theme. We should not be any more vexed by what happens to our material possessions than the lawyer was by what happened to his Porsche.

One Step to Financial Freedom

Sitting at the coffee shop of the local Barnes and Noble bookstore, I glance up and see the New York Times' bestsellers arrayed in rows. Leading the selections are two books by Suzie Orman, *Nine Steps to Financial Freedom* and *The Courage To Be Rich*. Next to them is a shelf containing recommendations by the staff of the store, including *The Seven Habits of Highly Effective People* by Stephen Covey. These books (and many others like them) dispense a strange combination of economics and spirituality. They promulgate the view that financial prosperity and spiritual well-being are linked, that getting your spiritual house in order actually pays financial dividends. One of the titles is especially revealing: *God Wants You To Be Rich*.

It's an odd view, one that certainly runs counter to approximately 2,500 years of spiritual and religious thought, both Eastern and Western, in which financial and worldly success is generally viewed as an obstacle to the spiritual path. This is not to say that the type of thinking these books are advocating is wrong, but rather to point out that we should perhaps be a little skeptical of joining together two concepts that have traditionally been viewed as incompatible—as is the case with losing weight and eating chocolate. To be sure, Christ's statement that it would be easier for a camel to pass through the eye of a needle than for a rich man to enter the kingdom of heaven has been interpreted by some as a metaphorical claim not to be taken at face value. But it is not the only injunction in the Bible which hazards a warning about wealth.

6 Chapter One

Such proclamations on the danger which money poses to spirituality are also not unknown in other religious traditions.

It is therefore not surprising to find that the first passage in the summary of Epictetus' teachings, known as *The Handbook*, contains a discussion of precisely this point. If you attempt to attain both worldly success and spiritual growth, Epictetus warns, you will probably achieve neither. Rather, if you aspire towards the life the Stoics advocate "you will have to give up some things entirely and defer others for the time being."[2]

Common sense leads us to side with Epictetus and Christ over Suzie Orman and Stephen Covey. Most of us know that building great wealth is a rare achievement, and that it requires a combination of determination and daring—and no small amount of luck. It should come as no surprise, then, that all religious traditions view the achievement of the spiritual life as equally demanding, and, in fact, more difficult than walking a razor's edge. Given that each of these goals presumes what amounts to a superhuman amount of effort, what are the odds of the same person achieving both? It is true that one may become a world class violinist and an Olympic athlete, a Nobel prize winning physicist and a great actor. But more likely than not, achieving even one of these ends will require a life's effort.

I suspect that books such as Orman's and Covey's are the result of a peculiar contradiction in the American psyche. We admire financial success in this country, so much so that, in a magazine article, it was recently speculated that the definition of an American might well be "someone who wants to be rich." However, it is also important to note that 95% of us believe in God. That a tension exists in the human psyche between the spiritual and the material paths is hardly an insight. What is novel is the belief that the contradiction is illusory, that the path to spiritual progress and financial achievement is one and the same. By dressing up greed in a spiritual garb and implying that there is no price to be paid for the examined life, these new books are following an old path, one taken by every diet plan that says you can lose twenty pounds in a week, and every financial scheme that claims you can make a million dollars with no money down. Stoicism leads us in a very different direction in so far as it declares that the spiritual life has a cost and that in all likelihood part (but by no means all of it) will be financial.

In order to be truly liberated, we must rid ourselves of delusions. It is the truth, as the saying goes, which will set us free. If Stoicism is correct, then a first truth about the relation between material wealth and spirituality is that they are inherently opposite in nature, and any philosophy that promises everything without a price tag can only be specious.

Show Me The Money

Having mentioned earlier that, at least theoretically, Stoicism is not incompatible with the possession of extensive material belongings, I pointed out that what makes one a Stoic is an attitude of non-attachment towards possessions. From a practical perspective as well, however, it is next to impossible to concern oneself with amassing a great fortune while pursuing the spiritual life.

Recognizing this, Stoicism calls for a particular attitude towards material wealth. Stoics do not, as one might first believe, insist that we adopt a vow of poverty in order to devote all our spare time to the spiritual life. As it is our nature to be social, so it is our duty to contribute to the public good. Stoics were expected to be parents, citizens and neighbors; hence, a life of poverty was not viewed as a realistic option. But it was not that they didn't recognize the value of such an existence. Just as we might wish to emulate Mother Teresa or Gandhi—however unattainable their lofty ideals might be—so the Stoics esteemed people like the Cynic Diogenes. The Cynics, so named because their life appeared dog-like to the average citizen, lived in the open air, carried everything they owned, and begged for food. Diogenes' scorn for wealth and his rejection of pretense was legendary. Informed by Alexander the Great that he would grant him any request, Diogenes merely told the most powerful man in the world that he wished him to move a little to the right, for he was blocking the sun! The Cynics represented an ideal of self-sufficiency and independence that the Stoics felt was beyond the

Difficulties and Dissapointments

powers of most to achieve. And just as well. Its wholesale adoption would undermine any chance at a civic community.

But eschewing poverty does not license us to engage in the unbridled pursuit of wealth. Doing the latter is, as has long been noted, intrinsically unwise. That which human beings are most fundamentally in search of is happiness, and, contrary to popular conceptions both past and present, there is no necessary correlation between wealth and happiness. Moreover, once the pursuit of wealth has become a habit, the desire for it easily becomes insatiable. Like the mythical beast that sprouted several new heads for each one that was cut off, as soon as one desire is satisfied, others arise in its place: We are sure to need a bigger television, a newer car, or another vacation. Furthermore, having a substantial fortune leaves us vulnerable to the twists and turns of fate—and, at the same time, does not provide us with anything that truly enhances our well-being. Finally, even if we never actually lose it, the mere possession of a large sum of money significantly increases the general level of anxiety we experience in everyday life.

If neither wealth or poverty is right for us, then what is the right amount of worldly goods for us to possess? The Stoics were not romantic idealists. They recognized the role that money plays in our lives, and the fact that many of our troubles result from our relationship with our finances. But it is because they wished to minimize the impact it can have on us that they insisted on setting a limit to wealth–something we in the West generally fail to do. Be content with thrift, Seneca declares. Strengthen self-restraint, curb luxury, temper ambition, view poverty calmly, cultivate frugality.[3] Elsewhere he is more forthcoming: "In money matters the best measure is not to descend to poverty nor yet be too far removed from it."[4]

This might seem a bit extreme, but the fact is that most of us have more than we need to survive comfortably. What drives us and causes ceaseless irritation is the desire for more, and to counter it we should keep in mind Seneca's cheerful refrain: "How little a man requires to maintain himself. And how can a man who has any merit fail to have that little."[5]

A Fool's Paradise

When I was a child, we would go on vacation once a year, for about a week, to northern Wisconsin to visit my mother's sister in Peshtigo, about fifty miles north of Green Bay. It seemed like it took an eternity to get there, though now I know that it can be driven in less than five hours.

There wasn't a whole lot for my brother and I to do once we arrived. Mostly, I think, we stayed in the house and watched television. There was a pinball machine in the garage at which I spent numerous hours, but I don't otherwise have a lot of fond memories from my time there. No fishing, hiking, or hunting—nothing like that. I do recollect being awakened by singing one night after my parents, my mother's two sisters and their husbands returned home from dinner. That may have been my first explicit exposure to adult intoxication, though I'm not sure I was aware of it as such at the time.

And, none too soon, it was time to go home. At some point during the return journey my father would get tired, pull off the road, and drive around until he spotted a satisfactory hotel. As soon as we got into the room he would open up his little black case containing two bottles of liquor—one of brandy, the other of sweet vermouth—and mix a couple of Manhattans for him and my mother. There was usually a pool at these places in which my brother and I would swim, and a restaurant where the family would invariably wind up at dinnertime.

But that was more or less the sum total of events on our vacations.

Difficulties and Dissapointments 11

It's not exactly a Dickenisan story, but also not a particularly memorable one. The result was that I entered adulthood in a state of vacation deprivation, and didn't really have the money to begin my own adventures until I turned thirty and got my first full-time teaching job. I've known people who have been in long, loveless marriages, and when they divorced were determined to make up for lost time by hopping into bed with anything that moved. And it's fair to say that I behaved in pretty much the same manner when it came to vacations: I became a travel addict. Not wanting to bore you with the details, I'll just say that I've journeyed quite a bit since then, though neither wisely nor too well. My method was to get out of town as often as I could for as long as I could, and I was just as likely to take a camping trip to Yellowstone as to fly to Athens on a whim.

My experience may not be unique. Our culture seems obsessed with travel. It's available and affordable as never before. Travel magazines have proliferated, as have web sites. People don't seem content with simply flying off to Europe either. Adventure travel to the ends of the earth is the latest trend: Safaris in Africa, trekking Nepal, mountain biking in China. It's hard to object to all of this without suggesting that one is jealous to some degree. Yet there does exist a thoughtful contingent of people who refuse to be part of this trend. "Traveling is a fool's paradise," said Emerson. The *Tao Te Ching* adds, "The further you go, the less you know." The Stoics would take issue with this mania as well.

Seneca writes of meeting a young man who reports to him, with disappointment, the results of a long journey he had recently undertaken. The troubles he had hoped to escape from had followed him to every port, and he laments that he was unable to achieve the sought after peace of mind. No wonder he was unhappy on his trip, Seneca comments; he had himself for company.[6] I've come across numerous such travelers on my sojourns, and doubtless have been guilty of this discontent myself. More often than not, we choose to travel because of a weariness with life, a sense that we simply need to escape and a vain hope that things may look better or at least different upon our return. Sadly, the world we venture back to looks remarkably similar to the one we left; we arrive home not only bereft of financial resources, but drained of physical, emotional and spiritual energy. As Seneca reminds us, "If you really want to escape the things that harass you, what you're needing is not to be in a different place, but to be a different person."[7]

Society is constantly sending us messages to the effect that we need to buy something or go somewhere in order to be happy. To the extent that our desire to travel is motivated by the belief that travel is a necessary component of a full and complete life, we pin our chances for happiness on something outside of ourselves. This, according to the Stoics, is a fatal error. Perhaps when this urge to run hits, we should make a special point of sitting still and trying to change ourselves instead of our location.

On a Run

It was Friday morning, and I was out for a run. It was an early spring day, and after the long dead of winter things were just starting to come to life. The sun was shining, a gentle breeze with a hint of warmth was blowing, and buds were beginning to appear on the trees. Zipping along on a trail that looped around a golf course tucked against the side of a mountain, I was in a running zone, completely in accord with my surroundings and feeling especially grateful to be alive. It is times such as these, when everything seems right with the world, that I've discovered you really need to be on the lookout.

Up ahead I saw an older man with a bushy white beard working on the trail and perspiring quite hard. Next to him was a brown runt of a dog lashed to a tree. Experience has taught me not to startle people by shouting out, "Runner coming." Instead, I have found it best to make some noise: a cough, a kick at the dirt. Usually this is enough. People get the message and move aside. Following protocol, I made my usual sounds. The dog barked, the old guy gave me a glare, and everything seemed O.K.–until I tried to pass them. He not only refused to step aside but actually blocked my path. And then, as if talking to a six year old, the man looked me right in the eye and said, "Do me a favor. Next time you come up to someone working on a trail, announce yourself and then walk by."

My first impulse was to ask him if he would do me a favor and stick that shovel, well, somewhere in the immediate vicinity. But, instead, I

14 Chapter One

simply looked at him quizzically and ran on. When I was further down the trail, I congratulated myself on not blowing up at him. But I still could not shake the feeling of righteous indignation. I had indeed announced myself and he had seen me. But since I hadn't played the game by his rules, he was going to make me pay, even though what I did was perfectly good trail etiquette. The son of a bitch.

I ran a bit longer, but my mind kept going back to that jerk on the trail. I knew that my run would be ruined unless I could let this thing go. How we handle a slight, perceived insult, or flippant remark, says a good deal about who we are. Marcus Aurelius gives a list of guidelines (incorporated into the discussion below) on how to behave when one feels offended. It is somehow reassuring to know that this sort of thing was a problem even for a Roman emperor!

First, he said that we ought to recognize the natural kinship that exists between ourselves and all other humans. This may go some way towards mitigating against anger, since it is harder to be mad at a relative than at a stranger. Second, he suggested that we keep in mind that people's characters predispose them to act the way they do: "Consider what kind of men they are at table, in bed, and so forth: and particularly, under what compulsions in respect of opinions they are; and as to their acts, consider with what pride they do what they do."[8] If we can acknowledge that individuals are victims of a chain of circumstances going back to their childhood and even beyond, that, given who they are, they can't help do what they do, our rationale for feeling angry will dissipate. Third, Aurelius tells us to keep in mind that, "A man must learn a great deal to enable him to pass a correct judgement on another's actions."[9] Since we simply do not know what circumstances or pressures are weighing upon the individual who has offended us, it might not be out of line to give our fellow human the benefit of the doubt. Moreover, he advises us to be cognizant of the fact that it is not a given deed or action that bothers us, but rather our reaction to it. "Dismiss the judgment about an act as if it were something grievous, and the anger is gone."[10] Finally, if all else fails, we should remember "that man's life lasts only a moment, and after a short time we are all laid out dead."[11]

The goal, after all, is to maintain your mental equilibrium. Epictetus drives this point home when he says that we would not turn over our body to just any person we happen to meet.[12] Should we not be ashamed to hand over something more precious, our peace of mind, to someone who stumbles in our way?

Stoics in Love

Perhaps no human emotion seems more antithetical to Stoicism than love. Stoics, who distrusted any violent emotion, definitely disapproved of the frenzied state many of us identify with this term. Yet, the subjective feeling of being completely overwhelmed by passion and swept up in a romance is certainly one of the sweetest sensations life has to offer. Few of us are strangers to it. Not coincidentally, it is also the theme of a seemingly limitless number of Hollywood movies, television shows, dime novels and popular song lyrics. Thus, by disparaging love, Stoics seem to be running counter to both individual experience and popular culture.

But, if we are honest, we will admit that there is something to be said for Stoic skepticism on this topic, too. Hollywood hype is hardly reality, and the portrayal of love in the mass media equips one poorly (or maybe not at all) for the rigors of a shared, lifelong experience. While they offer an unending variety of romantic storylines and are quite ingenious at depicting complications lovers often overcome in order to be together, television and movies are notorious for failing to provide details on what happens after the happy couple says "I do." At most, the viewers are left to infer that the partners live blissfully ever after. But to promulgate this simplistic notion is about as useful as equipping someone for an African safari with a fly swatter and a Swiss army knife! It is, therefore, no surprise that when the excitement of the initial stages of romance fades, as it invariably must, those weaned on

16 Chapter One

the popular images of love are understandably disillusioned. Often, they go in search of another lover, hoping to recapture their earlier ecstasy, only to find that in time the glow wears off of that relationship as well. For many, this is a lifelong pursuit, an endless, sad cycle that contributes in no small way to this country's high divorce rate. In light of all this, the Stoic claim that the popular conception of love is in need of some serious revision, does indeed, I would propose, deserve our attention.

What the Stoics offer to counter this, however, may not initially sound very appealing, for they see marriage as nothing less than a duty required of us by nature, one of the nails that holds together the framework of society. When we hear such talk, we immediately call to mind images of cold, emotionally detached individuals who merely engage in relationships out of a sense of obligation. There is, however, nothing to suggest that this is the natural outcome of the Stoic view. Epictetus explicitly cautions that "we should not be unfeeling like a statue."[13] Moreover, duty is not necessarily passionless. Indeed, the devotion that can arise from a decision motivated in this way is evidenced by the innumerable lives laid down on the battlefield. It does not seem too much to suggest that there exists an intimate connection between fulfilling our obligations and living a meaningful life. This is nowhere more true than in marriage, which, by all accounts, can be one of the most fulfilling, and certainly one of the most challenging, experiences we are capable of undergoing.

To be sure, duty is not without its demands, and there are invariably times when obligation seems onerous and our desire to extricate ourselves from it strong. A new military recruit endures a physical regimen of early morning rising and enforced hikes that he would balk at as a civilian. But, in accord with the Greek proverb, "all good things are difficult," a feeling of achievement results from having subjected oneself to such discipline. Similarly, the Stoic attitude toward marriage—namely, that it is a profound obligation—will make one much more likely to remain in a partnership through its inevitable ups and downs, and thereby also increase one's chances of reaping great rewards.

There is yet another way in which an attitude of Stoicism can help marriages to endure: It raises doubts about the cogency of one of the most common reasons people walk away from them. While it is something of a truism to claim that people leave marriages because they are unhappy, it is also the case that they often blame their partner for this

Difficulties and Dissapointments 17

state of affairs, believing sincerely that, with someone else, things would be very different. Something like this is to be expected, of course, since it is human nature to attribute responsibility for our difficulties to others. We get a speeding ticket and rail against the police, faulty road signs, other speeding drivers—everything except our own inattentiveness. And, while it is true that in some circumstances, especially in cases of abuse, abandoning the other person will help secure one's own well-being, it is more often the case that a person exits a marriage only to be confronted with the same difficulties in an ensuing relationship. In other words, we may find ourselves forced to admit that we ourselves were the primary cause of our problems.

By emphasizing the notion that nothing external can cause a person's unhappiness, Stoicism forces the individual to confront this common marital difficulty in a very different fashion than is commonly done today. Assuming responsibility for the unpleasant situation, a person would first examine what it is about themselves that is causing them to experience problems in the relationship. If they are honest, they will find that there is much that they can work on internally. Only after having thoroughly dealt with our own inner turmoil are we in a position to seriously consider the proposition that leaving the other person is really necessary. But by the time most people reach this point, they discover that they can indeed find happiness within their current relationship—and the need to leave it is thereby eliminated.

Nothing the Stoics have to say, I think, should be interpreted as impugning the power and beauty of romantic love. Nor is there anything to suggest that they would disagree with the Greek view that love is a God (Eros). Indeed, they do not so much condemn romantic love as ignore it. Truth be told, they have a different agenda. Perhaps their strategy is best understood by assuming that they have in mind the same target audience as Aristotle did when he declared that no one under thirty-five was fit to listen to his philosophical discourses. By this stage of our lives, we can probably stand to be lectured about the virtue of keeping our commitments through difficult times.

The Last Day of the Rest of Your Life

Sometimes, Stoic writing can seem genuinely morbid. Epictetus says that whenever you kiss your wife or child, remind yourself that you are kissing a mortal"[14]–hardly something we want to think about when sending our children off to school in the morning. But, in reality, it may not be so far-fetched. While they are finishing their Pop Tarts and Minute Maid orange juice, the morning paper on the table testifies to the fact that people unexpectedly die every day, and for no particular reason. Evidently, someone was recently killed while standing in line for a ride at Disneyland. At Disneyland? For God's sake...

What are we to do in the face of such obvious evidence that death can always be immanent? We can dwell on it, as the depressive does, until we are psychologically paralyzed. Or, we can attempt to hide from it as most Americans today do, shipping off the old and infirm to rest homes, and trying as much as possible to cover up our own mortality with everything from plastic surgery to hair loss treatments. Stoicism, however, takes a different approach. It openly acknowledges and confronts death in an attempt to diminish the power it has over us, and even uses this knowledge as a means of enriching our experience of life.

One way to begin this process is by asking what we would have left undone or been lacking for a complete life, were we to die tomorrow. Only a fortunate few can reply to this question by saying, "Nothing." Many others would recite a surprisingly similar list of things they were planning on getting to someday: Travel, a different career, another

Difficulties and Dissapointments 19

partner, et cetera. There is nothing wrong with such a list, but, again, the Stoic simply refuses to see anything external as relevant to a full a complete life. Their view that changing something outside of ourselves will not fundamentally improve our condition is all too often validated when we do actually get what we thought we needed—the trip to Paris, the job in Seattle, the new romantic interest—and then find, much to our dismay, that something is still missing.

But the desire for external goods involves us in a never ending cycle. Once we decide that the good is outside of ourselves, it will, by definition, always be beyond our reach. Indeed, we have, in effect, reversed the order of things when we look to outward circumstances as either the source of, or solution to, our problems. The 19th century Danish philosopher Soren Kierkegaard humorously characterized this predicament as one in which someone is standing on the steps of the state capitol with his back to the building pointing directly in front of him saying, "There it is, there is the capitol." The observer is indeed right, notes Kierkegaard. He just need to turn around. So, too, the Stoic thinks we need to shift the focus inward, toward our state of mind and our character. These are the only things we have control over, and, for the Stoic, happiness can be found only in so far as we develop the proper attitude towards them.

The Stoic emphasis on death therefore serves to facilitate this inward turn and to focus our attention on what is truly important. Epictetus says, "Keep before your eyes day by day death and exile, and everything that seems terrible, but most of all death; and then you will never have any abject thought, nor will you yearn for anything beyond measure."[15] If, for example, we knew this to be our last day on earth, would we really get upset with trivial distractions? Would we not instead be kind to others, gentle with ourselves and grateful towards the universe? This, in essence, is the view of Marcus Aurelius. He tells us that "the perfection of moral character consists in this, in passing every day as the last, and in being neither violently excited, nor torpid, nor playing the hypocrite."[16]

Far from being morbid or depressing, this emphasis on death may in fact be a necessary step in our achieving true psychological wellbeing.

Suicide and Stoics

Many people have pointed out several areas where Stoic and Christian thought intersect–disdain for external goods, a recognition of the importance of controlling the passions, and an emphasis on our obligations towards others. This should come as no surprise, since historically Stoicism exerted a good deal of influence on the development of Christian ethical thinking. But Stoicism, of course, is not Christianity, and nowhere is this more apparent than in their respective attitudes towards suicide.

The Christian view on suicide is unambiguous: Taking one's life is wrong, always and everywhere. Since life is a gift from God, only He can revoke it. We have no right to hasten the process. This attitude is not unique to Christianity. Almost 400 years before the birth of Christ, Plato expounded a similar view on this subject. Furthermore, this blanket condemnation of the act of suicide also makes euthanasia unacceptable, since, in most cases, it is equivalent to assisted suicide. But, on this point, many Christians diverge from Church teaching, believing that, when death is immanent, the sort of prolonged suffering we see all too often today in hospitals and nursing homes can in no way be intended by a benevolent Deity. The relatively widespread support for the work of Dr. Jack Kervorkian among believers and non-believers alike is understandable under these circumstances.

In its own way, the Stoic view on suicide is as unequivocal as is the classic Christian one: Suicide is not only permitted but sanctioned by

God. "Above all," says Seneca, assuming the Divine persona, "I have taken pains that nothing should detain you against your will; the way lies open. If you do not wish to fight, you may escape. Of all the things which I deemed necessary for you, therefore, I have made none easier than dying."[17] Stoics, who disagree about the interpretation of numerous doctrines, are, however, in accord on the permissibility of self-murder. "This is why not one of the things that befall us in life is a difficulty," explains Epictetus. "For whenever you wish, you may walk out of the house."[18] Marcus Aurelius echoes this sentiment when he says, "As you intend to live in the next world, so it is in your power to live here. But if men do not permit you, then get away out of life. The house is smoky, and I quit it. Why do you think this is any trouble?"[19]

The ease with which these men talk about suicide causes many to recoil. It seems not only to be sacrilegious but also to represent a callous disregard for life. In fact, I want to argue that the Stoic attitude towards suicide is at least as reverent as the Christian view and equally as life affirming. It is also, I think, more in line with modern sensibilities that would permit euthanasia and grant individuals more autonomy over their existence.

Traditionally, Western religions have viewed suicide as an affront to God, an attempt to override His will. But to say that we must not kill ourselves because God has intended that we endure our fate is to hold God responsible for the particulars for the lives of each and every existent thing. Such an attitude may increase our respect for God's power, but it is not without its drawbacks. If our thinking implies that God is the cause of a great deal of seemingly senseless pain, a certain level of resentment is generated towards the Deity. By contrast, the Stoic view of the Divine imposes no such burden on God. Although they view God as the creator of the universe and the ultimate source of our existence, Stoics do not wish to sully God with the details of individual destinies. Instead, the Stoic God delegates responsibility—to us. In particular, he equips us with Reason in order to determine when this existence is truly unbearable. And since he did not assign any of us our personal fate, he also does not require me to remain in this world at all costs. Rather, the decision to either stay or leave is ours. By refusing to ascribe to God control of individual lives, Stoics offer us a picture of the universe that cannot logically generate any ill-will towards the Deity.

There are, however, other reasons why the Stoic view of suicide seems equally as respectful of life as the Christian one. Stoic principles do not assert that we may destroy ourselves at the least provocation, or

22   Chapter One

that mere inconvenience or discomfort justifies our taking out lives. Instead, we have significant duties to our family, friends, and country, and to mankind in general, from which we may not easily extricate ourselves. Epictetus chides one man for shirking his responsibility by running away from home when his daughter was ill. So, too, there exists a myriad of claims on our energies, and these claims bind us to this earth. In the Roman Empire, in particular, where Stoicism flourished, suicide was often carried out in order to protect one's family from an emperor's retribution. Socrates, a model suicide in their view, drank hemlock in order to avoid violating his central moral beliefs. As these cases demonstrate, only circumstances which could be truly described as extenuating were viewed as justifying suicide in the minds of the Stoics.

That having been said, one cannot read what the Stoics have to say on this subject without realizing that cases other than those which involve great physical suffering would warrant suicide. Yet, it is far from clear that sanctioning a practice increases its likelihood any more than condemning it succeeds in preventing it. If history has taught us anything, it is that prohibitions are rarely effective. Consider, for example, the great resistance to America's ban on alcohol in the 1920's, or, also, a recent report which stated that abstinence-only programs are less effective at preventing pregnancies than those which included discussion of contraception. Once a subject is taboo, its appeal is, of course, irresistible. But, just as bringing a forbidden subject into the open can also result in a generally healthier attitudes toward it, so adopting the Stoic stance on suicide might actually have the effect of preventing some cases of it. Moreover, and though it may seem peculiar, contemplating suicide can be an oddly invigorating experience, and with regard to this, the Stoics have at least one religious author on their side. The Catholic novelist Walker Percy, no stranger to depression, counseled that if every other treatment failed one should try imagining that one has killed oneself, and look upon the time that remains as a bonus. Marcus Aurelius dispenses exactly the same advice: "Consider thyself to be dead, and to have completed thy life up to the present time; and live according to nature the remainder which is allowed thee."[20]

The agreement between these two thinkers gives us some reason to believe that the Stoic and Christian traditions may not diverge as radically on this point as initially claimed. After all, it is possible to attain similar ends by disparate means. Far from being disrespectful of life, then, allowing suicide under certain circumstances may in fact go no small way towards the Christian goal of enhancing its sacredness.

The Golden Years

A specter is haunting America—the specter of the baby boom retirement. Apparitions are already looming on the horizon. Commercials for the American Association of Retired People show active seniors splashing in the water and speeding down the highway in convertibles. Ads for a large investment firm depict retirees riding their bikes across a rugged landscape. And the newspapers recently report a flurry of arrests in Arizona of seniors for having sex in public.

Some find this trend encouraging. In a culture that glorifies youth and has lost the belief that elders are a source of wisdom, the concept of mature adults acting like teenagers is certainly understandable. We all want to be like the most popular kid in school, so it is no surprise that the persons whom society most readily ignores should attempt to mimic those getting all the attention. And it is not only with respect to activities, but also personal appearances that the old copy the young, as the booming plastic surgery industry illustrates.

Still, there is something forced, something desperate and even something a little pathetic about trying so hard to be something we are not (for the young will always surpass their elders at being young). As Seneca so indelicately puts it: "Aren't you ashamed to be wanting and working for the same things you wanted when you were a boy?"[21] These words, written to a correspondent, reflect the Stoic idea that the last part of life should be occupied with different concerns than the earlier stages. In their view, the lifestyle described at the start of this essay is not one to be recommended to seniors primarily because it goes against nature.

24   Chapter One

While the body necessarily deteriorates with age, the mind and the spirit can continue to burn bright. Perhaps, say the Stoics, nature is telling us to turn our attention to those things that are still strong in us, toward the more metaphysical aspects of our being, and live a life in line with those values. Seneca spent his later years precisely in this way:

> I have buried myself away behind closed doors in order to be able to be of use to more people. With me no day is ever whiled away at ease. I claim a good part of my nights for study. I have withdrawn from affairs as well as from society; I am acting on behalf of later generations. I am writing down a few things that may be of use to them. I am pointing out to others the right path, which I have recognized only late in life, when I am worn out with my wanderings.[22]

As the first paragraph of this essay indicates, the portrait of reflective old age is not the prevalent image today. However, the notion that we become more inward later in life is not exclusive to the ancients. The Swiss psychiatrist Carl Jung echoes the same sentiment:

> But we cannot live the afternoon of life according to the program of life's morning; for what was great in the morning will be little in the evening, and what in the morning was true will at evening have become a lie. Aging people should know that their lives are not mounting and expanding, but that an inexorable inner process enforces the contraction of life. For a young person it is almost a sin, or at least a danger, to be too preoccupied with himself; but for the aging person it is a duty and a necessity to devote serious attention to himself. After having lavished its light upon the world, the sun withdraws its rays in order to illuminate itself.[23]

The suggestion that our elders turn to reflection and contemplation rather than to travel and adventure might seem to suggest only that they should be further marginalized—removed to an even greater degree from the mainstream of life. In fact, I believe the opposite is the case, and that the peripatetic lifestyle illustrated at the start of this essay is a recipe for disaster. If elders are simply treading the same path as the young, but doing so at a slower pace, then youth has no more reason to pay attention to them than one would to someone who has fallen behind

Difficulties and Dissapointments

in a race. After all, one feels only pity for slowpokes. But if the aged are on a different journey, an adventure of the soul and spirit, then we have reason to look for them for guidance on a road we will all tread. Hence, the more reflective approach to old age advocated by the Stoics is not only the key to more self-satisfaction at this stage of life, but is also crucial to restoring our elders their honored place as guides and mentors.

In Sickness and in Health

Imagine the following scene: About fifteen students crowd around a large table in a small, windowless seminar room. The instructor walks in. As usual, the students have left one side of the table empty, and he takes his seat there. He looks particularly out of sorts this morning and lets loose with a rather loud sneeze shortly after putting down his books. A dialogue unfolds as follows:

Instructor: Don't worry, I'm not contagious. [He pauses to blow his nose]. We were scheduled to talk about Stoic ethics this morning. But I have something more important I want to discuss today. I have a cold.

Student 1: That's more important than Stoic ethics?

Instructor: Perhaps not. But it's my class. Besides, you certainly would agree that how we handle sickness is an aspect of Stoic morality.

Student 1: Yes.

Instructor: Then I think I have a real live question of more than theoretical interest. We're all somewhat committed to Stoicism in this class. And we're all going to get sick at some point. So let's try to come up with some Stoic guidelines for dealing with ill health, if for no other reason than that I could really use them right now. I've brought some passages we can discuss. But why don't you first give me your general impressions. What

Difficulties and Dissapointments 27

should a poor Stoic with a cold do?

Student 2: I'm not exactly sure why, but it doesn't seem to me a Stoic would go around announcing he has a cold. [general laughter]

Instructor: You're right Jeff. Let's listen to a passage in which Marcus Aurelius quotes from Epicurus: "In my sickness, my conversation was not about my bodily sufferings, nor did I talk on such subjects to those who visited me."[24] What do you think? Sound like good advice?

Student 2: Sure, and I wish more people would follow it. It seems to me most people, when they get sick, feel compelled to tell you all about it. And in more detail than you really care to hear.

Instructor: So, Stoic Rule #1 in dealing with sickness is not to talk about it. Why do you think that's a good idea?

Student 3: Well, no one really wants to hear how sick you are. So it's an imposition on others.

Student 1: So?

Student 3: Stoics feel you have a responsibility to be of use to others and not to burden them.

Instructor: Precisely. My concern for others could by itself motivate me to be silent when sick. Is there any other reason it might be a good idea not to talk about your illness? [silence] Forget about others for a second: Are there any reasons it might not be in your interest to talk about your illness?

Student 1: One thing I've noticed is that talking about your illness causes you to focus on it.

Instructor: And what's wrong with that?

Student 1: Well, it seems to me that the worst times of an illness are when you're aware of it, for example, lying in bed simply feeling miserable. It's much better to be absorbed in something and so lost in it that you forget you're sick: Writing, reading, or something like that. Talking about your illness is more like lying in bed thinking about how sick you are. It just makes you feel worse.

Student 2: What about talking about not talking about your illness?

Instructor: I don't think I want to go there. Let me continue with the rest of the quote. "Nor did I give the physicians an opportunity of putting on solemn looks, as if they were doing something great, but my life went on well and happily."[25]

Student 3: Now that sounds crazy.

Instructor: Why?

28   Chapter One

Student 3: It just doesn't seem realistic to be bogged down with a cold and go on "well and happily." I get this picture of someone whose nose is running while they're skipping down the block whistling.

Instructor: Granted that is one way to go on well and happily, though it's never been a particular habit of mine. But what else might those words mean?

Student 1: I think all it means is that you act as if you don't have the cold. You don't change your routine.

Instructor: Is that possible?

Student 1: Sure. I've known people who, well, you just don't know that they're sick. They show up to work, they go to the gym, they don't miss a beat. But then there are others—most people really. It takes over their lives. They miss classes because they sleep in. They use it as an excuse to not do anything. And you know what? The people who don't give into it simply seem to stay sick for shorter periods of time and get sick less often.

Instructor: So can we list as Stoic rule #2: Don't change your routine.

Student 3: But shouldn't you take care of yourself? Get plenty of rest, drink plenty of water, et cetera? And what about going to the doctor? The passage we quoted recommends that we basically disparage doctors. But, if you have something contagious and you don't get antibiotics, you're going to get a lot sicker—and you might make others sick, as well. So I'm not so sure it's good advice just to continue your normal routine and not do anything differently.

Instructor: Good points. But let me deal with the second one first. Epictetus did not know about antibiotics, but I think it's clear also that he would not want us to endanger the health of others. So, if going to a doctor would help make us less contagious, we probably have an obligation to do so. Keep in mind, however, that one real medical problem today is the overuse of antibiotics. People who stop using antibiotics, or take them when they're not needed are contributing to the creation of super-viruses that could fell a rhino. So perhaps the Stoics are right to be a bit suspicious of running to the doctor. Now as for taking aspirin, getting plenty of rest and drinking liquids, I don't see that those are inconsistent with having life go on its normal way.

Student 2: But why should a Stoic take any steps to get better, even rest

Difficulties and Dissapointments 29

and liquids? Isn't health what Stoics call an 'indifferent'?

Instructor: Yes, it is. Stoics do not see health as a good, nor do they see sickness as an evil. Remember, though, that, for them, some of the 'indifferents' are preferable to others.[26] Certainly our physical well-being can affect our ability to perform our duties and hence also our ability to be virtuous. If we are so sick that we can't get out of bed, then our ability to do good is certainly diminished. Hence, the Stoic has some reason to prefer health over illness. It is also the case for the Stoic that to be healthy is a more natural condition than illness–and hence more preferable. However, in their view, there is nothing morally good in and of itself about being healthy—a fact which we need to clearly understand.

Student 1: But, consider people who go to the gym regularly. They think that the healthier, fitter, and more muscular they are, the better they are as persons. They look with disdain at anyone who appears the least bit flabby or overweight.

Instructor: Yes. Our culture certainly promotes this attitude. Epictetus talks about faulty reasoning at one point, i.e. moving from the claim 'I am richer than you' to the conclusion 'I am better than you'.[27] Our culture seems to have done this with respect to physical appearance—slenderness, in particular. 'I am fitter than you' implies 'I am a better human being than you are'. And, so, when the Stoics say that 'health is an indifferent,' their point is that the state of your health in no way affects your moral status or personal worth. This is a lesson we might take to heart. We can also include a third notion: "Take the minimum amount of self-care necessary for getting better." When you have a cold, taking vitamin C hardly seems excessive, nor does getting a little extra rest, though people generally go overboard in this category. And, yes, since there is a duty not to harm others, the use of antibiotics would not be ruled out, either.

Student 2: It sounds a bit like Aristotle's golden mean?

Instructor: In a way, yes. Remember, however, that when Aristotle says that virtue lies in a mean between two extremes, he is claiming that it is usually more noble to lean towards one of the extremes. Consider, for example, the virtue of courage. One can be cowardly, or one can be overly rash and reckless in situations of danger. Courage is the mean between these two ex-

30   Chapter One

tremes. But if you are going to err, Aristotle declares, you're better off leaning more towards being rash and reckless. I think we can say the same thing about taking care of ourselves. There is such a thing as overindulgence—doing nothing but staying in bed once we get sick—and there is also what he would term recklessness, running outside naked at ten below zero when we have a cold. We need to find a balance between these. But if we are going to err, we ought perhaps give too little rather than too much attention to our health.

Student 3: Maybe another thing which a program of not changing our routine can refer to is our relations with others. It's easy to be irritable and short-tempered when you're sick. We have to make an extra effort to watch how we relate to them during times of illness.

Instructor: Yes. Just like we would compensate for driving on an icy road by going more slowly and being more careful, so, too, when our physical health has been disrupted, we might have to take extra care in our interactions with others, work to maintain an attitude of congeniality and avoid varying routine unnecessarily.

Student 2: But, all of these rules—not talking about our sickness, not varying our routine, taking a minimal amount of self-care, being especially cautious in our interactions with others—refer to external actions. For the Stoics, it is our thoughts that are of primary importance, not our actions, since they are all we have ultimate control over.

Instructor: Good point. All these actions would, however, have to spring from the proper state of mind. In other words, we won't feel compelled to talk about our illness if we don't *judge* it to be a bad thing. We won't vary our routine or take excessive care of ourselves, because we *judge* that nothing extraordinary is happening. All of the actions we have discussed spring naturally from the achievement of a state of mental equanimity.

Student 1: But you know, it is not just simple health problems, like colds, that raise this question of self-discipline. Sometimes, we get a serious flu and really can't get out of bed. And sometimes it is even worse—a lot worse.

Instructor: Yes, of course. And Epictetus was no stranger to the fact that one can be simply be incapacitated by illness. "Like a stroll, a voyage, a journey, such also is a fever. I presume you

Difficulties and Dissapointments

do not read while taking a stroll, do you?–No.–No more than when you have a fever."[28] So there are indeed some things we aren't able to do when we're sick, and that has to be taken into consideration. But dealing with such things is precisely what we have been training for as a Stoic. We shouldn't balk at enduring an illness any more than an athlete would run from competition. Remember, whatever happens to us externally can form no part of our essential nature. What matters is how we react to challenges and difficulties. Epictetus talks about how to be sick in the right way.

Student 3: Really? So, not only do I get sick, but I am also expected to somehow do it in the right way?

Instructor: Only if you want to be a Stoic.

Student 3: O.K., let's suppose I do. So, what exactly does that mean?

Instructor: I'm glad you asked.

> What does it mean to have a fever in the right way? Not to blame God or man, not to be overwhelmed by what happens to you, to await death bravely and in the right way, to do what is required of you, when your physician comes to see you, not to be afraid of what he will say, not to be carried away if he tells you the news is good and not to be downhearted if the news is bad.[29]

Student 3: Well that sounds, ah, pretty stoical.

Instructor: Precisely.

DESTRUCTIVE EMOTIONS

Little Things

Having heard too many tales of lost luggage, and having even experienced a few of the resulting inconveniences myself, I almost always carry my bags onto a plane. It was with great reluctance, then, that upon returning from a family visit over Christmas, I checked through a suitcase full of gifts—and did so knowing that I would have to hurry to catch a shuttle home after we had landed. Since ours was a relatively short flight with no changes, I was fairly confident that the timing would work out. Shortly after we arrived, I was able to retrieve my bag; however this was still not sufficient. When I reached the ground transportation desk, I was informed that I had missed the last scheduled bus (by less than a minute), and would have to scramble to find some other way home. It was late in the day and also the end of a long holiday. I was tired and had classes early the next morning.

We all have experienced countless situations like this, when a schedule we had planned was derailed for reasons we could not possibly have foreseen. They occur with such frequency it almost seems as if someone is conspiring to do this to us, and, though such situations often amount only to minor inconveniences, they add up: the missed bus, the lost credit card, the car you didn't know needed repairs—all these incidents take a noticeable toll on us. Even routine activities like shopping, getting the oil changed, or cleaning the house can cause resentment. By this I do not mean the pleasant things like cooking a good meal, but rather driving to the market, or the waiting in the checkout line to buy

36   Chapter Two

food. These are situations with which we would rather not occupy ourselves, because we are, effectively, powerless to change the fact that they consume precious time and result in annoyance, frustration and boredom. The Stoics, however, had a good deal to say about such moments.

Probably the most famous piece of Stoic advice on this topic is Epictetus' paradoxical claim: "Do not seek to have everything that happens happen as you wish, but wish for everything to happen as it actually does happen."[1] That is, we should act as if we had actually willed any event which takes place, no matter what it is. If we adopt this attitude, he says, our lives will go well. This idea may sound defeatist, and may seem to suggest a refusal to take responsibility for what occurs, but, in fact, there is a lot of wisdom in Epictetus' suggestion that we "ought not to lead events, but to follow them."[2]

We can all readily observe that getting angry at something that has already occured is a totally fruitless activity–there is no benefit to be gained from it whatsoever. Fretting and fuming don't change anything. There is also the fact that rage is bad for us, both physiologically and psychologically. Hence, in so far as it requires us to alter our attitude towards an unpleasant experience, Stoicism directs us towards a healthier mode of being.

But, is it realistically possible for us to act as if we had willed some unfortunate circumstance, for example, and to not be upset but actually pleased by this event? "Yes," says Epictetus: "Everything has two handles, by one of which it ought to be carried and by the other not."[3] By this he means to drive home the obvious but often overlooked fact that it is completely within our power to decide whether we will fret and fume or remain calm.

Of course, such acts of restraint are much easier to talk about than they are to carry out. The devil is indeed in the details. Fortunately, Stoicism offers us an array of strategies designed to aid us not only in remaining calm, but also in developing a sense of gratitude toward some seeming disaster. The first of these involves examining the event for what good it might contain. If we choose this approach, it is up to us to become creative interpreters of reality. The lost wallet may well remind me I have too many credit cards, or that I place too much emphasis on material things. The foot injury may serve as a sign for me to slow down. In other words, the goodness or badness of a given event is for the most part not set in stone. It is a truth we create, not one we discover. Two people can experience the same flight delay and describe it in such different terms that the listeners will wonder if they were even on the same planet, much less in the same airport. One may have used

Destructive Emotions

the extra time involved to read an inspiring magazine article, have a conversation with an interesting person, or, even just watched the sky change color at sunset and describe it with such fine detail that it calls to mind a painting by Monet; the other may have complained about the heat, railed against the crowds and lamented the loss of time. Although both will have found themselves in the same circumstance, their judgments about it will diverge radically, thereby forcing us to conclude that the delay itself had no intrinsic meaning, and that it was neither good nor bad, but rather that assessing its impact was, in the end, the business of each of the individuals involved.

Second, if, after careful scrutiny, we cannot find a concrete benefit in a given situation, we still do not need to admit that it either caused or constituted a misfortune. Instead, we can declare in all honesty that since we cannot see into the future, the experience may well prove beneficial at some later point. Far from being driven by delusion, this sort of thinking strikes me as an honest admission of our cognitive limits and a recognition of the fact that things we thought were bad at the time often have proven to be quite the contrary–and vice versa.

Finally, even if it seems impossible that a given situation can yield any benefits at all, we should still not dismiss what is happening as entirely lacking in value. Rather, we ought to construe all such events as part of a learning curve. "When a difficulty falls upon you remember that God, like a trainer of wrestlers, has matched you with a rough opponent. For what purpose? Why that you may become an Olympic victor, which is not accomplished without sweat."[4] While it is easy to be calm when things are going well, we can only develop as human beings by maintaining our composure in difficult situations. Perhaps we ought to regard self-control as a prized possession that we can display at particular times, the way others might show off a pair of hiking boots or a new watch.

Instead of encouraging us to dwell on our helplessness, Stoicism insists we focus on the power we actually do have in a given situation. Whatever the circumstances, we can utilize our imagination and self-control and thereby remain in good spirits. It has to beat the alternative.

Edith Piaf, Stoic

Regret. It seems to involve feeling bad about a choice made in the past, for example, a decision to move, leave a spouse, or resign a job. Or, it can stem from an action that was hurtful or caused harm, an opportunity squandered, a road not taken, a word not said. Rare and fortunate is the individual unfamiliar with this phenomenon, the person who can sing with Edith Piaf "Non, Je ne Regrette Rein" ("I regret nothing"). Instead, regret seems to be the psychological equivalent of the common cold. We are all susceptible to it, and all too often. And, just as it is possible for a cold to develop into pneumonia if we don't monitor it closely, so, too, the sum total of these regrets can paralyze us on our current spiritual journey if we are not careful.

In this context we are reminded of the old Rubik's Cube. It was always difficult to get all the parts aligned correctly, although some people seemed to be able to do it with ease. Similarly, with respect to our lives, we sometimes examine the fragmentation and discord that seems to prevail in them, wonder how things became such a mess and speculate on the diminishing possibilities of achieving the harmony we once imagined. This is the victory of regret. Stoicism is no stranger to regret. Indeed, Epictetus says it should teach "how a man may rid his life of cries such as 'woe is me' and 'wretch that I am'."[5]

How do we do this? Stoicism doesn't ask us to deny our feelings or accept the palliative that everything happens for the best. This latter position was lampooned sufficiently by the French philosopher Voltaire

Destructive Emotions

in his novel *Candide*, in which the title character undergoes a series of personal disasters only to be reassured by his theology professor Pangloss after each new trauma that, despite appearances to the contrary, this is indeed the best of all possible worlds. The emptiness of this strategy becomes especially apparent when we actually apply it to a given situation by, for example, telling someone who has just lost her job, been sentenced to prison, diagnosed with breast cancer, or had a marriage fall apart, that everything happened for the best. There may be crueler, more thoughtless things to say, but most of us would find ourselves hard pressed to think of them. Indeed, the fact that a strategy cannot be employed precisely where it is needed gives us serious reason to doubt its soundness. It is as if we approach a sick patient with some means known to cure his or her ailment, but then claim it would not be applicable in this case.

Stoicism confronts us with the task of examining any situation to determine what good it can produce—a task that may sound a lot like this medical predicament. However, there is all the difference in the world between deluding ourselves into thinking an event happens for the best (even though we have no idea what that may be), and the process of scrutinizing what might seem like a bad situation to find in it some realistic and realizable benefit. The former is a thoughtless stance that can be mimicked without understanding, requires no intelligence and, at the end of the day, produces nothing of any consequence. By contrast, when properly applied, the latter strategy—which utilizes reason, deliberation and a good dose of realism—can change a life.

The importance of our attitude towards any situation is well illustrated by Viktor Frankl, a psychoanalyst who spent World War II in Nazi concentration camps. In his book *Man's Search For Meaning*, Frankl explains that given precisely similar external circumstances, some of his fellow prisoners were crushed while others survived. The determining factor, Frankl concluded, was attitude. While the majority of prisoners completely abandoned hope and simply vegetated, some accepted the situation as presenting a challenge and an opportunity for inner victory. It was no coincidence, argued Frankl, that those who took for the former path perished in higher than usual numbers.[6]

A good friend of mine was electrocuted and suffered third-degree burns over half her body. Strong and physically active, she was reduced to near immobility by the accident, and no one would have blamed her had she sunk into a state of despair. However, she took a decidedly different approach to the situation. She began to contact relevant organizations, communicate with other burn victims and establish a network of individuals who found themselves in similar situtaions. Before long, she was volunteering with a company that taught communication skills to burn victims, and even editing a newsletter on the topic. The last I heard she was planning to spend part of a sabbatical working with the group, which is located in England, and was ultimately hoping to found a chapter in the United States.

Such an accident could never be construed as having happened "for the best." Having seen her hover near death, undergo several years of painful surgeries and struggle through rehabilitation, I would regard such a claim as ludicrous. However, she has triumphed over her circumstances–and maybe there is nobler goal in life than this.

We can view the past with regret or gratitude; we can face the future with fear or courage; we can exist in the present with a disturbed mind, or live out our days in a state of personal equanimity. If the latter was possible for those in concentration camps, surely it is attainable for most of us.

Perhaps we would do well to take the advice of Marcus Aurelius:

Be like the promontory against which the waves continually break, but it stands firm and tames the fury of the water around it. "Unhappy am I because this has happened to me." Not so, but "Happy am I, though this has happened to me, because I continue free from pain, neither crushed by the present nor fearing the future. For such a thing as this might have happened to every man; but every man would not have continued free from pain on such an occasion."[7]

Fear and Loathing in Stoicism

The Art of Happiness is the result of a collaboration between a Western psychiatrist and the Dalai Lama, an extended interview in which the spiritual leader of Tibetan Buddhism attempts to present his system in Western terms and demonstrate how it can speak to us today. At one point in the work, he is explaining the difficulties he encountered when trying to understand one particular psychological term. When he was initially introduced to the notion, he was baffled. Not only was there no parallel concept in the Tibetan language, but the very idea seemed incomprehensible to him. On reflection, he was sure he must have simply misunderstood the speaker, but was then assured he had not. And, when it was finally explained to his satisfaction, he was more saddened by the knowledge that the phenomenon existed than he was delighted to have grasped the concept of *self-hatred*.[8] Sadly, there seem to be few of us today who are in the Dalai Lama's position. The number of hours spent on the therapist's couch, the quantity of Prozac ingested and the pure bulk of self-help books published all testify that many of us are none too comfortable with ourselves.

Many attempt to blame religion for the problem. Does Christianity not teach us that we are insignificant in comparison to the Divine? How can such a worthless creature have any sort of self-love? This does not, however, seem to explain the phenomenon of self-hatred, and there are two reasons why we ought not to accept it. First, there is the historic fact that the Stoics confronted this problem well before Christianity

42   Chapter Two

became a dominant influence in thought about ethics. Its roots must therefore run deeper. A second, more important reason to reject the claim that religion is responsible for this problem is, however, that a more plausible explanation may be much nearer at hand.

Even if one is hesitant to go along with the current trend of media-bashing, one has to admit that many of the complaints about the media, especially television, are not without merit. Daily, we are bombarded by images of lives that seem better than our own. We are not as beautiful as the people on the screen; we do not own as many nice things, or have the same interesting experiences they do, et cetera—and therefore come to feel dissatisfied with our lot in life. Not coincidentally, advertising on such programs highlights the products we need to purchase in order to make ourselves better, happier people. But, of course, purchasing them never really produces the desired result. Buying things will never make us feel good about ourselves, nor will it ever bring us any closer to living the life of a screen star. The new convertible really will not get the girl. Instead, the cycle of raised expectations and dashed hopes perpetuated by the media propels us into a downward psychological spiral which, I would argue, ends in the pit of low self-worth which the Dalai Lama found so difficult to comprehend.

Attributing the cause of such a negative course of personal development to religion would be like blaming a rainstorm in another country for the flooding that occurring in one's basement—and doing so while staring at a burst pipe. Sometimes the answers to our questions are entirely obvious! A recent article in *Psychology Today* illustrates this well. It was entitled "Why I Hate Beauty," and was written by someone working for a successful advertising agency in Hollywood. The author of the piece laments his inability to find a lasting and satisfying relationship, and blames this situation on the fact that he is being constantly exposed to beautiful, unattainable women through his job. Those with whom he could realistically develop a relationship interest him no longer—they pale in comparison to the super models he encounters daily.

So, too, we denigrate our own situation when confronted with one that seems obviously superior. The modest but perfectly acceptable life we are currently living begins to seem inadequate when compared with the "Lifestyles of the Rich and Famous" witnessed daily on television. Instead of counting our blessings, we torment ourselves with thoughts of our inadequacies.

Marcus Aurelius wonders "how it is that every man loves himself

Destructive Emotions 43

more than all the rest of men, but yet sets less value on his own opinion of himself than on the opinion of others,"[9] and Epictetus says it is the goal of Stoicism "to contrive how you may have no mean thoughts about yourself."[10] Clearly, then, the Stoics were not strangers to this troubling phenomenon. And, if they mention it, then neither Christianity nor contemporary advertising can be entirely to blame. It might instead be explained by the existence in us of some sort of demon bent on undermining our self-worth. The media certainly seem to aggravate and intensify its effects, but it may be an inherent part of our make-up–the ineluctable dark side of the personality that we must confront in order to achieve psychic health, just as we must overcome a natural tendency towards laziness in order to gain physical well-being.

The remedy that the Stoics offer for this condition of low self-worth is an age-old one, but it is no less useful for this reason. A connection to a principle larger, more enduring than ourselves lies at the core of all true spirituality. Indeed, systems as diverse as Buddhism, New Age metaphysics and fundamentalist Christianity recognize both that there is something permanent anchoring our existence and that we gain strength from a connection to this source. Even contemporary secular humanism casts its lot with humanity, and, in so doing, recognizes a meaning larger than itself. Despite the differing rationale for these systems, the result of an association with a transcendent force is clear: it provides us with nothing less than our sense of the sacred. If we achieve this mental attitude, we might marvel at the universe in rapt wonder, or contemplate all life with bemused satisfaction, or even shake our heads in utter bewilderment. But we will never doubt that existence is inherently meaningful, and hence will have no reason to call into question our own value.

Stoic thought taps into this tradition, relying on the notion of an eternal, transcendent force governing the universe as a way to infuse ourselves with a sense of purpose and meaning. Marcus Aurelius nicely sums up the Stoic views on the Divine (which I'll talk more about later): "There is one universe made up of all things, and one God who pervades all things, and one law, one common reason in all intelligent animals, and one truth."[11] If you accept the doctrine that your very presence in the universe connects you with this principle, Epictetus declares that "you will never have any ignoble thoughts about yourself."[12] It is important to point out here that the Stoic God is not, like the Judeo-Christian God, a separately existing Being, but is instead best understood as a rational ordering principle infused throughout the cosmos. To be sure, there is a good deal more to the Stoic conception of God than what these passages suggest. However, introducing metaphysical distinctions can sometimes distort the simple and powerful truth that some connection to the Divine, however we understand it, is the most efficient way to save ourselves from the overwhelming sense of insignificance that many people (ourselves included) would inflict upon us.

Keeping Company with the Abyss

A friend of mine practices what she calls the Lake Bonneville meditation. Lake Bonneville is the name for the ancient body of water that once covered most of the area of what is now called Utah. The Great Salt Lake is but a tiny remnant of it. She directs an arts program at a local university, and is always struggling against the odds to get funding or to find audiences for high quality productions that often go unnoticed. She is also a liberal Democrat in the most Republican state in the union, and a confirmed agnostic in an area thoroughly dominated by religion.

Whenever things get to be too much for her, when the forces of evil appear to be triumphing, she brings to mind a particular image in order to calm herself down, namely, the return of Lake Bonneville. She envisions the waters slowly rising above their current boundaries, covering the freeways, the houses, and the shopping malls, working their way up to the mountains which once formed their natural shores, ultimately overwhelming the landscape and returning everything to its original state. When the visualization is complete, a peace descends upon her which plays no small role in getting her through the day.

Doubtless, this sort of existential frustration is something we all encounter from time to time. Instead of imaging the return of Lake Bonneville, which may not do much for you, let me recommend a copy of the *Meditations* of Marcus Aurelius, which offers a liberating dose of the same medicine. It's what I call "keeping company with the abyss,"

46 Chapter Two

reminding ourselves of the ultimate insignificance of all things. The emperor-philosopher tells us, for example, to "think of the rapidity with which things pass by and disappear."[13] He asks us to "consider the universal substance, of which you have a small portion; and of universal time, of which such a short interval has been assigned to you".[14] And he reminds us that "Asia, Europe are mere corners of the universe: all the sea a drop in the cosmos; all the present time but a point in eternity."[15]

Such thoughts are interspersed throughout the *Meditations* like speed limit signs on a highway, and it is worth reflecting on their purpose, for the philosophical work of dwelling on the ultimate meaninglessness of all things can easily be misguided. Such mental and spiritual exercises are, however, not unique to Stoicism. The Biblical Book of Ecclesiastes espouses essentially the same message: "Vanity of vanities," it famously begins. "All things are vanity. What profit has a man from all the labor which he toils under the sun? One generation passes and another comes, but the world forever stays."[16]

But, such a view of life may be harmful and engender a dangerous nihilism. If nothing matters, why bother to put forth any effort whatsoever? Why even take the trouble to go on living? These are of course questions every mature person must answer and, as Camus reminds us, there is no truly healthy individual who has not contemplated taking his own life. One thing is, however, certain, namely, that we do ourselves no favor in hiding from the ultimate insignificance of all things. To begin with, it is simply a fact that in the larger scheme of things none of our efforts will amount to anything, and that it will not be long before all we do is forgotten by our descendants and, ultimately, by time itself. (Anyone contemplating immortality through art would be well advised to ponder the fire at the library at Alexandria).

A more important reason to spend time reflecting on the vanity which attaches to human affairs, may, however, be that such reflection can be oddly bracing. Far from depressing us, such thoughts can provide the perspective that is needed to get through the days with a modicum of sanity. This is precisely what Marcus Aurelius points out:

> You can remove many things that disturb you by comprehending the whole universe, and by contemplating the eternity of time, and observing the rapid change of all things, and how short is the time from birth to death, and the illimitable time before birth as well as the equally boundless time after death.[17]

Stoic Grief

One never sees the problems associated with one's own views. That's what friends are for. So, it shouldn't have been surprising that the most impassioned objections raised against the ideas these essays contain were raised by someone who should have been sympathetic to them: A fellow philosopher well-versed in Stoicism.

The charge began with the story of a mutual acquaintance who had lost his long time companion to AIDS. How, I was asked, would the Stoic have consoled the bereaved? What words would Epictetus, for example, have offered in an attempt to assuage this most bitter of blows? And, how would the Stoics have those of us who are merely observers respond in such situations? Surely, a philosophy should be judged by how it contends with these most weighty matters, just as the merit of a leader is assessed by how he reacts in a crisis.

As I was preparing my response to these challenges, my colleague began his own reply. When a philosopher asks a question, it is not always for the sake of receiving an answer. Before I knew it, my colleague was quoting Epictetus.: "If you kiss your own child or wife, say to yourself that you are kissing a human being; for when it dies, you will not be disturbed."[18] "Never say 'I have lost it' but instead 'I have given it back'. Did your child die? 'It was given back'. Did your wife die? 'She was given back'."[19] "When you see someone weeping in grief at the departure of his child . . . take care not to be taken away by the appearance that he is suffering something bad. What weighs him down is his

48   Chapter Two

judgment."[20]

Summing this up, he then said: "According to Epictetus, we are supposed to treat our loved ones like a twelve-pack of returnable bottles and insist that everyone else does likewise. I guess that at the memorial service tears were entirely inappropriate; we were all supposed to sit there like stones." And, by way of conclusion, he asked, "How can a philosophy that is so disconnected from life possibly be of any value to us?" Before I had a chance to respond, another colleague chimed in. He was undergoing a painful divorce after a twenty-year marriage. Although he agreed with the notion that physical objects contribute nothing to our well-being, he was a bit disturbed that we were being advised to treat humans in the same manner. "A car is one thing," he said, "a human being is quite another."

At this point, it was necessary to interrupt since the discussion was getting out of control. The listeners were becoming irritated and, more importantly, the meaning of Stoicism was being distorted. In truth, however, this should not have been surprising. This was an age-old charge, one that had been leveled at Stoicism since its inception, namely, that it is a cold and heartless philosophy detached from life as most of us actually live it. Nothing could be further from the truth. Looking carefully at the original texts demonstrates this clearly, whereas facile interpretations can often distort the system's true intent.

I. Gratitude for Life, not Indifference to Death

> If you kiss your own child or wife, say to yourself that
> you are kissing a human being; for when it dies, you
> will not be disturbed.

It is easy to misinterpret the meaning of this statement by viewing it as being self-serving in nature, merely intended to ease the blow when a loved one dies. Such a strategy, which is aimed at preventing further suffering, is clearly prudent in many areas of life. For example, it makes sense not to become too attached to material possessions, or to a current occupation or favorite past time. Jobs—even academic jobs—are tenuous affairs, physical objects disappear for a variety of reasons, and injuries may spring up to permanently disable one. By not investing too much of oneself in such transitory things, one may better be able to weather their loss. But there is a deeply troubling contradiction here: To treat human beings in this way is not only unacceptable, but morally

Destructive Emotions

repugnant. Clearly, we ought not deal with the loss of a child as we would the theft of an automobile.

For the Stoics, the point of keeping before us thoughts of the mortality of a loved one is not to diminish the importance of their death, but rather, to wake us up to the present moment and its possibilities. "Did you enjoy everything in which you took delight as though you were to enjoy it forever?" Epictetus asks his audience at one point.[21] Many of us do, indeed, take the present moment for granted and are almost shocked when friends depart for other jobs, children leave home, or aged parents die. If we had anticipated such events and truly dwelt on their inevitability, as Epictetus asks us to do here, perhaps we would not have left anything unsaid or undone–and therefore would feel less regret when departures and losses actually do occur.

"What keeps you from loving a person as one subject to death?"[22] Epictetus rhetorically asks his audience at one point; and what he means is not that we should anticipate someone's demise, but that we should cherish that person's presence. By asking us to be fully aware of the possible loss of those we love, Stoicism actually provides us with a valuable tool for remaining more awake and alive in the context of our relationships.

II. Spiritual Maturity, not Emotional Cruelty

> Never say 'I have lost it' but instead 'I have given it back'. Did your child die? 'It was given back'. Did your wife die? 'She was given back'.

It is perhaps no stretch to say that, more than any other, this quote may be responsible for the bad reputation the Stoics have sometimes been accused of having as regards human grief. The calm they would have us cultivate and demonstrate in the face of personal tragedy may initially suggest that theirs is a philosophy which does not acknowledge human emotion at all and is therefore devoid of basic respect for life. Grief, someone once said, is the tax we pay for loving. If we don't grieve, can we truly be said to have loved?

The first thing to note here is that the seemingly hardened attitude towards grief evidenced by Stoicism is not unique among the world's spiritual traditions. The Hindu epic *Bhagavad Gita* relates the story of the warrior Arjuna who is distraught at having to go to war against his kinsmen. He is told by the god Krishna not to grieve because the world

50   Chapter Two

is illusory in nature—one ought not put too much stock in it, or in transitory events like life and death. Buddhism presents us with the tale of a woman mourning the loss of her child and coming to the Buddha for advice. Before he will counsel her, he insists that she go into town, find a household that has not suffered a death, and bring him back a mustard seed from that home. When she returns empty handed, she realizes that her plight is universal. Nor is it only in Eastern thought that we find such an attitude of seeming indifference toward death. When a young man says that before he can join Christ he must bury his father, Christ replies, "Let the dead bury the dead."

In urging us to handle death with equanimity of spirit, Stoicism is following a long tradition—one that counsels a fundamentally different attitude towards it than might seem natural. The point is not to emotionally numb ourselves, but rather to begin to develop spiritual maturity. It insists that we reject the childish demand that events in life proceed as we wish them to, and accept that death is part of the fabric of life. Needless to say, this is not easy advice to follow. However, none of the world's spiritual traditions assert that life is easy. The First Noble Truth of Buddhism declares that life is suffering, and Marcus Aurelius observes that the art of living is more like wrestling than like dancing, to which Epictetus adds that "each man's life is a campaign and a rather complicated one at that."[23]

But there is more to the Stoic attitude towards grief than merely accepting it as a hard fact of existence. Life is not a veil of tears for the Stoic. At the core of this philosophy is, rather, a sense of gratitude. To someone bemoaning his inability to travel to the far reaches of the globe Epictetus remarks, "Wretch, are you not content with what you see daily? Have you anything better or greater to see than the sun, the moon, the stars, the whole earth, the sea."[24] A similar sense of the grace of the everyday ought to characterize our attitude towards our loved ones. If we view the human beings who cross our path as gifts from a greater source than ourselves, then it seems that, rather than grieving their loss when it does occur, we can celebrate their life and be thankful for the portion of it allotted to us.

Everything, as Epictetus says, has two handles by which it may be grasped. This is to say, grieving is not a necessary corollary of loving. Confronted with loss, we may also adopt a stance of gratitude, reflecting on the joy that the universe has given us through the being of the other. The choice of what to focus on is, as the Stoics remind us, entirely up to us.

III. Stoicism and the Suffering of Others

> When you see someone weeping in grief at the depar-
> ture of his child . . . take care not to be taken away by
> the appearance that he is suffering something bad.
> What weighs him down is his judgment about the
> matter.

Whereas the previous quotes spoke to the Stoic attitude toward personal loss, this one seems to indict Stoicism for its callous indifference towards the suffering of others. At first read, it appears that Stoicism is telling us to discount the real pain of someone dealing with the loss of a loved one–what is unfortunate is not what has happened to the grieving parents, but rather their opinion about the matter. Several points need to be made concerning this. First, the saying is addressed to the Stoic himself as a reminder of how he ought to behave in a given situation. Far from being unmoved, the Stoic is very much affected by the plight of parents who have lost a child, and he must remind himself not to get carried away.

Should we then criticize the Stoic's resolve not to get upset or lose his equilibrium? One could instead make the case that losing control is beneficial neither to the individual nor to others in such a situation. The extent to which emotional upset and breakdown in the face of others' deaths is psychologically healthy is certainly an open question. Although it may be something of a given today, in an era in which we confess our innermost secrets on national television, that one needs to "show one's feelings" and "not keep it in," certainly other ages and other extant traditions have viewed the matter differently. Hence, retaining equanimity of spirit may not only be possible but actually beneficial for one who is himself faced with grief. Moreover, in most any emotionally charged situation, a calm and controlled person can undoubtedly be both a source of strength and a sense of calm for others. The Stoic, then, sees no reason why either his own well-being or that of others should be threatened under such circumstances.

But it is equally important to note that he also does not require others to adhere to his standards, nor does he judge them for their failure to do so. That is, the Stoic would never chastise grieving parents for inappropriate behavior. Instead, as all the evidence suggests, he would go out of his way to take into consideration the feelings of others.

Chapter Two

Epictetus advises someone whose friend is grieving "to not, however, hesitate to sympathize with him so far as words go, and, if occasion offers, even to groan with him; but be careful not to groan also in the center of your being."[25]

One might criticize the Stoic for acting hypocritically in displaying tears merely in order to assuage the grief of a friend or mother. Doing so, however, would be unfair. First, we often do express ourselves less than honestly in various social situations. If, for example, the daughter of a good friend were getting married, and I happen to have several legitimate reasons for disliking the groom, it would be inappropriate for me to express these concerns at the ceremony. Such discretion is not deliberately deceptive, but is rather merely part of the flexibility which we, as flawed human beings, are compelled to exercise if we are to live together. The Stoic's 'crocodile tears', if they may be called that, are shed in the hope of alleviating real and legitimate suffering. In other words, it is hard to see how a well-intentioned act which harms no one and which concerns nothing other than my own belief system can warrant any sort of moral condemnation. Surely, an atheist can encourage a dying relative's belief in God if doing so will ease suffering—something which can, in fact, be done without any degree of insincerity or hypocrisy.

The Stoic's approach to grief is therefore very different than that which he is commonly (and often incorrectly) understood to be advocating. Although he chooses not to display what we might call the traditional signs of mourning, he is certainly moved by human suffering. His choice to retain composure while others may break down is a personal one, and it seems hard to criticize even if one cannot adopt it. Who can say conclusively what constitutes a right or a wrong approach to loss? At least the Stoic does not make any effort to impose his views on others—and he also does whatever is in his power to alleviate their suffering. What could be a more respectful gesture toward others?

Emotionally Intelligent Stoics

Stoics are often accused of being emotionally dead, of attempting to replace the complex and often contradictory world of emotions with cold, calculating reason. Epictetus tells us that "no good man laments or groans or weeps"[26] and counsels us to "cast away sadness, fear, envy, desire and malevolence."[27] The good Stoic, we are told, will feel "no pain, no anger, no compulsion" but instead will live "in tranquility, free from perturbation."[28] Depicted in this way, the Stoic seems (at least to us moderns), to be cut off from the passions and concerns that motivate us and make life worth living. It is for this reason that many find the Stoic ideal not only unattractive, but psychologically unhealthy.

Recent work on emotional health, however, echoes certain of the Stoic claims. In his book *Emotional Intelligence*, Daniel Goleman makes a convincing case that how we handle our passions is at least as important for success in life as any innate intellectual ability, since the quality of our emotional life is at the heart of a meaningful existence. But this does not come by luck or birth. It results instead from training and can therefore be nurtured and taught. In what follows, I want to explore the various ways in which Goleman's discussion of emotional health parallels Stoic thought.

The first trait of emotional intelligence for Goleman is self-awareness, an ability to step back from a situation even as it is taking place.[29] Most of us fail miserably at the task of observing ourselves in this way. Instead of distancing ourselves from a stressful event, more often than

54   Chapter Two

not we respond with knee-jerk reactions. Somebody cuts us off on the highway, and we get angry. A spouse says a hurtful word, and we answer in kind. Although we might admit in retrospect that our behavior was irrational, and often wish we had acted differently, we somehow find ourselves unable to do so in the moment when it is necessary. For Goleman, the key is self-awareness. Being aware of any psychic unpleasantness as it occurs invariably motivates in us a desire to extricate ourselves from a bad mood.

It is precisely this ability to step back from what is going on, to become at least temporarily a spectator to, rather than a participant in events, that lies at the core of the Stoic analysis of experience. Stoics point out that our emotional reactions are invariably preceded by some motivating incident. The examples noted here, namely the *actions* of the bad driver and the *words* of the vindictive partner, occur prior to the outburst and seem to provoke it. Stoics ask us not to respond to these stimuli immediately, but, instead, to examine the situation and, in the words of Epictetus, to "put it to the test."[30] This test is a simple one: We need to ask ourselves what is within our control and what not. The driver's swervings and my spouse's words are obviously not within our control—people will drive as they wish and say the things they want. If an event is not within our control, say the Stoics, it only makes sense to give no more thought to it and instead focus our energies on what is within our grasp, for example, how we respond to a trying situation. Doing otherwise would be comparable to knowing the winner of a race in advance and not betting on it.

In contrast to the Stoic method of examining events before reacting to them, most of us are, as Epictetus notes, "always adding something to appearances and representing them as greater than they are."[31] If a spouse has to go to the dentist for a thousand dollars worth of work that is not covered by insurance, we fret and fume about how we are going to pay for this. By adding something (my reaction) to the problematic event (the dental work and its cost), we upset ourselves and perhaps strain our marriage, transforming another speed bump on the road of life into a crisis situation.

But how can we break the seemingly iron link between our experience of an event and our response to it? The key, as Marcus Aurelius tells us, is to keep Stoic principles to mind: "As physicians have always their instruments and knives ready for cases which suddenly require their skill, so should you have principles ready for the understanding of things divine and human."[32] When someone cuts us off in traffic, we

Destructive Emotions

pause before reacting and examine our probable response in light of Stoic doctrine: "When you are offended at any man's shameless conduct, immediately ask yourself, 'is it possible, then, that shameless men should not be in the world?' It is not possible. Do not, then, require what is impossible."[33] Or perhaps we can follow the guidelines on developing a larger perspective on such incidents: "Consider when you are vexed or grieved, that man's life is only a moment, and after a short time we are all laid out dead."[34] Or maybe we ought to contemplate "how much more pain is brought on us by our anger and vexation at offensive acts than by the acts themselves at which we are angry and vexed."[35] Reminding ourselves of these and other Stoic imperatives will go a long way towards helping us control our reactions and generally allowing us to stay a bit more sane.

A good Stoic, then, possesses self-awareness. He has mastered the art of stepping back from what is going on and controlling his reaction to events by invoking philosophical principles and focusing on the one thing that is in his power, his reaction to what occurs. This level of self-control is not achieved immediately, but rather through constant practice. "Pay attention to your impressions and watch over them sleeplessly," states Epictetus. "For it is no small matter that you are guarding but self respect, fidelity and constancy."[36]

Don't Worry, Be Stoic

A second characteristic of the psychologically healthy individual, according to Goleman, is the ability to control the more destructive feelings.[37] This amounts neither to simply repressing emotions, nor to ignoring negative states of mind, but rather to confronting such feelings head on and dealing with them in a rational manner. Goleman illustrates this point with respect to three particularly destructive emotions: anger, worry and depression. Generally, we admit that these psychological states have no positive value. Since they disrupt us psychically and wreak psychological havoc, it seems obvious that our lives would certainly be improved if we were able to diminish the presence and effects of any or all of them. It is the mark of the emotionally developed person to translate this widely shared aspiration into reality.

To illustrate how anger can be controlled, Goleman describes one experiment which took place at a gym.[38] The test subject was instructed to arbitrarily treat other members very rudely. As a result of this behavior, his fellow exercisers were visibly upset and, when given a chance to retaliate, readily did so. The experiment was, however, also conducted with some minor variations. He was, for example, called away to the phone at one point and it was explained he was undergoing great personal and family stress. Given this information, people generally calmed down and ceased their retaliatory actions. The moral of the story is that seeing things from the other's point of view can have a remarkably calming effect—one that those who are interested in anger man-

Destructive Emotions

57

agement would do well to investigate.

The Stoics offer two versions of this strategy of developing sympathy towards others as a way of heading off anger. One is somewhat limited in scope, and the other more global. They propose that we first imagine that a person who might otherwise evoke our anger is acting on behalf of a benign and even benevolent motive. The well-dressed driver who cuts into our traffic lane may be unemployed and late for an important interview; or, the woman standing in the checkout line with too many items may simply be trying to make it home quickly to a sick child. Although it might seem like wishful thinking, this creative interpretation of reality is grounded in an honest recognition of how little we really know of each other. As Marcus Aurelius points out, "A man must learn a great deal to enable him to pass correct judgment on another man's actions."[39] That is, if we give people the benefit of the doubt and assume that the motive for their less than noble actions is understandable, then we will go a long way towards preserving a degree of equanimity of spirit in ourselves—even if we are sometimes overly generous in our judgments.

Other cases, however, do not so readily admit of such a harmless interpretation, e.g., the car mechanic who overcharges us, the colleague who spreads lies about us, or the thief who breaks into our house. Unfortunately, most of us could provide a not insubstantial list of times we have been the victim of an unjust attack borne of ill will. If we haven't known the spite of Iago, we've had dealings with someone who seems to have studied under him. Here, Stoics ask us to confront a truth about human nature—one which is not so pleasant as that previously discussed, namely, that everyone thinks themselves completely justified in whatever they do. Men, as Marcus Aurelius puts it, act under the "compulsion" of their opinions about right and wrong, good and bad.[40] How they come to their conclusion involves a causal chain going back further than anyone can reasonably trace, but Stoics believe it is, in all likelihood, impossible for some people to have acted differently, given their background and level of development. Christ said the poor will always be with us; Marcus insists it is the impudent and stupid who are mainstay of the human condition. Given the inevitability of ignorance, bad training and wrong belief, it makes about as much sense to get angry at someone who wrongs us as it would to fly off the handle at an electrical appliance for not functioning.

It must be conceded that there are numerous differences between people and toasters. For example, toasters didn't contribute to their

58   Chapter Two

current condition while people invariably did, and hence bear at least some responsibility for who they have become. But the Stoic does not get angry at someone who has developed deficiently from a moral point of view any more than one feels rage at someone who is physically maimed. The proper reaction in these cases is sympathy and even pity, responses which, by and large, are inconsistent with justifiable anger. The Stoic strategy of reinterpreting motives, recognizing the inevitability of others' actions, and acknowledging that a level of moral deficiency is part of the human condition offers to those who wish to remain calm rather than indulge their anger an alternative method of dealing with troubling emotions.

Anger is a sporadic problem for most of us. By contrast, worry and anxiety seem to be chronic conditions in many people. No doubt, this is connected with the contemporary pace of life: We overextend ourselves, work too much, and have far too many commitments. This is all very understandable, but is it desirable? It hardly seems so. According to Goleman, worry is inherently problematic for emotional health. It contributes nothing positive to a situation and wholly undermines our ability to arrive at constructive solutions to the dilemmas we face.[41]

Of course it is one thing to tell someone not to worry, and quite another to actively reduce their anxiety. Merely repeating the words to the popular tune "Don't Worry, Be Happy" probably won't be very helpful. To inform someone that if he wants to be happy, then, in general, he shouldn't worry is about as useful as letting him know that if he wants to be rich he should make money. But what should we say to another in these trying circumstances? Unfortunately, there is no easy answer to this.

Stoics, who view reason as our greatest good, ask us to utilize it to deal with anxiety. While it is much more natural to give into our passion than it is to deliberate about emotions and submit them to examination, the Stoics require that we do indeed preoccupy ourselves with the latter task if we wish to conquer our sense of worry. First, they recommend that we radically alter the way we view the anxiety with which we are burdened. Often, people hold that the cause of their worry is an external event, some real or imagined state of affairs—the possibility of accident, a work deadline, sickness, divorce, job loss or death. But the Stoics remind us that this is an incorrect analysis of the situation. It is not the external event that is causing our anxiety; rather, it is our judgement of the situation.

Hence, if we wish to combat anxiety we need to examine our judg-

Destructive Emotions

ments and ask whether or not they are rational. The following case demonstrates this well: A car has stopped on the highway, so the driver gets out, lifts up the hood and stares inside at the engine, examining the various components in search of the possible cause of the problem. Before he can do anything, his wife points out that the gas tank was nearly empty yesterday and asks if he remembered to fill it up. He realizes he has not and almost immediately ceases his investigation of the car's engine. Under these conditions it would be irrational to continue; it is not only pointless but actually counterproductive–searching further prevents him from doing what needs to be done in order to solve the problem. Stoicism asks us to confront our thoughts with the same attitude of care and exactitude we would apply to the problem of trying to fix our Toyota, and hence also requires that we not expend energy unnecessarily or inappropriately, as we do when we allow ourselves to worry.

A perennial source of anxiety is money. Suppose that like many Americans we have managed to accumulate significant credit card debt and that this fact has been keeping us awake at night. What course of action would the Stoics prescribe in this situation? First, they would doubtless insist that we recognize that it is not the bills that are causing our insomnia but our reaction to them. And, while we can't wave a wand and make the debt disappear, we can undertake a process of rational deliberation to alleviate a good deal of the anxiety (as well as come up with a rational plan to begin eliminating the debt).

Debtors prisons do not exist, and unless we have been dealing with the mob, our creditors cannot physically harm us. Even our house is protected in bankruptcy proceedings. In other words, the situation of the person deeply in debt to credit card companies is not all that dire. We will eventually have to pay it off, and doing so might make things financially precarious for us a good while. But, what person of substance ever identified their well-being with their net worth? As Seneca reminds us, "How little a man requires to maintain himself. And how can a man who has any merit fail to have that little."[42] When viewed in rational terms, then, challenging life situations are not only manageable, but they also hold the potential for significant personal growth.

So we might conclude these reflections with a slight alteration on the popular song title, "Don't Worry, Be Stoic": Our judgment about the situation is the cause of our anxiety, we are in control of our powers of judgment, and any judgment we make must pass some minimal test of its rationality, as is the case with the malfunctioning car. Although this

60 Chapter Two

formula will probably never find its way into the words of any popular song, it can go a long way in loosening the hold which worry often has over our lives.

Of all the negative emotions, depression seems to be the most intractable. It often comes out of nowhere and just as mysteriously evaporates. In some cases, however, it can and does settle in and take over a life. Few of us have remained entirely untouched by the latter situation, whether through personal experience or that of a family member or friend. It is important to initially point out here that Goleman's advice is not intended for those serious cases which require medication and professional treatment. Rather, the situation we are dealing with here is what is termed sub-clinical depression, or what Goleman prefers to call ordinary melancholy—the blues that descend upon all of us from time to time.[43]

He begins with the assumption that, just as there are many preventative measures we can undertake to ward off physical illness, so, also, there are steps we can engage in at a psychic level that have similar prophylactic effects. According to Goleman, one of the most powerful tools we have at our disposal is "cognitive reframing," or, what we might colloquially term seeing the situation in a different light.[44] Rather than dwelling on the negative feelings that often accompany the break up of a relationship, we can, for example, reflect on what we have learned and contemplate with joy our new found freedom. A lost job can be viewed as pointing us in a fresh, new direction just as an accident or illness can be interpreted as providing a much needed rest.

In essence, the Stoics invented cognitive reframing. With one simple phrase—"Everything has two handles by which it can be grasped"[45]—Epictetus introduced a way of viewing experience that many still find fruitful some two thousand years later. Rather than descrying solitude, he declares "you ought to, when staying alone, to call it peace and freedom and to look upon yourself as like the gods." Instead of complaining about having to go to a party, you should "call it games, a festival, and try to keep holiday with the people."[46]

In conclusion, then, asking whether a state of affairs is adverse or propitious is not like trying to determine whether a chair is brown or black. The meaning of the situation is rather, to a large degree, the one I wish to give it. And, whether or not we interpret something as a setback or an opportunity for growth seems to be entirely a matter of the mental disposition of the perceiver. The Stoic strategy is, however, not without its limitations. Events such as the death of a child are clearly not susceptible to this treatment, and there are some whose minds are simply incapable of being affected positively by it due, for example, to some sort of chemical imbalance. But, if we are honest with ourselves, we will admit that much of life can be handled in this way, and that we will be better off to the extent that we are able to say with Epictetus': "Bring whatever you will and I will turn it into something blessed, productive of happiness."[47]

Tragic Optimism

Hopefulness, optimism, cheerfulness—in general, a positive mental attitude—constitutes the third characteristic of a healthy emotional life for Goleman. This basically involves having a strong expectation that things will turn out all right in life, despite setbacks and frustrations. Goleman presents a good deal of evidence to support his claim that besides being valued for its own sake, a positive state of mind yields results. A sense of optimism and hopefulness in students is, for example, a good predictor of academic success. A survey of 500 members of the incoming freshman class of 1984 at the University of Pennsylvania demonstrated that student scores on a test which measured the degree of optimism about the study experience were a better predictor of their grades than were SAT scores or high school grades. Another study revealed that salesmen who were more optimistic recorded better sales. Finally, a positive mental attitude has been seen for quite some time by many physicians to play a vital role in a patient's recovery process.[48]

Optimism may, however, not be the first word that leaps to mind when one contemplates Stoicism. One is much more likely to think of Marcus Aurelius's musings on mortality and his acknowledgment of the vanity of all things:

> Of human life the time is a point, and the substance is in a flux, and the perception dull, and the composition of the whole body subject to putrefaction, and the soul a whirl, and fortune

Destructive Emotions

63

hard to divine, and fame a thing devoid of judgement. And, to say all in a word, everything which belongs to the body is a stream, and what belongs to the soul is a dream and vapor, and life is a warfare and a stranger's sojourn, and after fame is oblivion.[49]

It suffices to say that the Stoics can never be accused of seeing the world through rose-colored glasses.

To be fair to them, however, we need to distinguish between two types of optimism. First, there is what might be called "simple optimism," a state of mind in which we naturally remain cheerful and upbeat under any circumstances. Consider, for example, two opposite types: The person who seems to constantly be living under a dark cloud and also the one whom we might describe as clinically cheerful. Either person's state of mind can seem puzzling and annoying to the rest of us, given that most of us seem to alternate between hope and despair, and, for the most part, to pass our days in a condition which is somewhere in the middle. But these "simple optimists" should perhaps be no more praised or blamed for this character trait than one is for having red hair of for being double jointed. They may merely be fortunate in so far as they possess a naturally sunny disposition.

By contrast, the state of mind characteristic of the Stoic might be referred to as one of "tragic optimism." Instead of seeing the world as constantly bathed in sunlight, this viewpoint acknowledges that darkness, too, is part of the fabric of things and declares that any abiding positive mental outlook must ground itself in this reality. In this, the Stoics harken back to their ancient Greek roots, where tragedy reigned as the highest art form. Although a fascination with these dramas may strike us as morbid here and now (in the land of the situation comedy), the Greeks seemed to have concluded both that tragedy accurately reflected the true nature of life and that recognizing this fact could be oddly bracing.

Any optimistic attitude worthy of the name must first confront the fact that darkness is also inherent in the human condition. Before our cheerfulness and lightheartedness can mean anything, we must acknowledge its polar opposite, shadow and gloom. This is why there is a world of difference between the smile of a child and one of a mature adult who has witnessed forty, fifty, or sixty or more years of life. If there is something touching about the simple optimism of the former, the latter strikes us as more truly valuable if only because we know it must have been proceeded by struggle.

This is the spirit of tragic optimism: To see through the weariness of life and conclude that, despite everything, all is well. This is why Seneca can prod his listeners to, "Learn how to feel joy."[50] Unlike what passes for joy in most people, the Stoic version of the emotion is the product of a sustained effort and lasts a lifetime. Since the Stoic knows he can remain unperturbed in all circumstances, he exists fully in the present moment: content with his lot, desiring nothing but what the days bring, grateful towards the gods, and well-disposed towards humanity.

Stoics in Society

The last two characteristics of an emotionally healthy agent relate to the quality of our interpersonal relationships.[51] The first trait at issue is empathy, the ability to know how another feels. Goleman points out that everything from good lovemaking to successful child rearing requires an attunement to the other's emotional state. Conversely, dysfunctional states of being such as alcoholism and depression manifest a pronounced lack of capacity for this. More important, however, is Goleman's claim that the roots of morality are found in empathy. It should therefore not be surprising to find that sociopaths are almost completely devoid of this emotion. Nevertheless, we must translate this empathy into successful relations with others. Not only will competency here have obvious implications for success in a variety of areas, from business to romance, but, if Aristotle is right in his claim that we are by nature 'political animals', then it makes sense that our emotional health would depend upon our being able to foster healthy human relations.

What exactly was the Stoic attitude towards their fellow humans? And, how does it compare to Goleman's prescription for empathy and good will towards others? They are often caricatured as cold, aloof individuals and stand in direct contrast to the caring and compassionate person that Goleman seems to hold as an ideal of proper psychological development. Once again, however, it should not be surprising to find that this caricature is a gross distortion of what the Stoic texts actually say.

66   Chapter Two

To begin, and for the sake of historical accuracy, it should be noted that Stoics are among the first in the West to develop the notion of universal compassion. Fidelity to one's tribe, city-state, or nation seems to have been the norm in the ancient world. The Stoics found such opposition between peoples false and unnatural. According to Epictetus, we all have Zeus as a father and are "born of the same seed."[52] This requires that we recognize a kinship, what Marcus calls the brotherhood of all rational beings. Indeed it was Marcus Aurelius who proclaimed "we are all fellow citizens . . . and the world is a single city."[53]

More important than this universal concern is the advice Stoics dispense about how to foster relationships in our daily lives. First, there are positive duties towards others. These start with the natural connections we have to certain people as a result of birth. We are sons or daughters and hence have obligations to parents, or we are brothers or sisters, and have obligations to siblings. There are also the non-familial bonds we forge with others. We have friends and certain responsibilities towards them. As a member of the species, we have some duty to perpetuate it, usually (but not only) by means of marrying and having children. In addition, we are residents of a political community, which entails what Epictetus called "the profession of citizen,"[54] and requires that we actively participate in the governance and management of society at all levels. It is evident therefore that, far from standing aloof from their fellow human beings, the Stoics were very much a part of the fabric of civic life.

Nor did they accept social responsibility reluctantly. That is they did not merely engage in social activity only out of a sense of duty, and find no real joy in the process, the way we might visit a sick but distant relative at the hospital. To the contrary, when Epictetus exhorts his students to "return to your country [and]...relieve the fear of your kinsmen,"[55] one gets the sense that Stoics are generally concerned for the psychic well-being of their fellow humans.

Rather than being isolated from others, or antagonistic or indifferent towards them, Stoics are actively engaged with others, concerned about their well-being and attempting constantly to generate good will towards them. It is hard to imagine a truly healthier way to relate to others than along the lines of this model.

Are Stoics Happy?

Some things really don't change. Almost 2,500 years ago Aristotle wrote that "both the general run of men and people of superior refinement say that the goal of all action is happiness."[56] Few would disagree with this today, but, even though we might endorse this claim, the majority of us could not be further from a genuine understanding of what constitutes happiness.

For most of us, happiness has at least two characteristics. First, we tend to view happiness as fleeting. We claim to be happy one day, sad the next, even ecstatic at one moment, and in the depths of despair soon thereafter. Second, we also ascribe to the tenet that our happiness depends, to a large degree, upon external circumstances. For example, almost everyone believes that if they were to win the lottery, their problems in life would be solved. On a more mundane level, we often assert that we are happy precisely because we have received a promotion, were mailed our tax refund, or enjoyed a nice vacation, et cetera. But assenting to such reasoning amounts to admitting that our psychological well-being is beyond our control. Had we owed all of our newly gotten gains to the government, had it rained on our trip, or had we been demoted or fired—elements not entirely up to us—we would have subsequently been miserable.

Aristotle and other Greek thinkers (including the Stoics) had, however, quite a different view of the matter. For them, our happiness was not really hostage to external factors, but came about instead as a result

68 Chapter Two

of a stable character—one that develops over time and by means of our own efforts. In other words, whereas many today see happiness as dependent upon things ultimately beyond our control, much of Greek philosophy asserted that happiness was determined by things inside of us and hence realizable by means of our own efforts: It is how we deal with things, not the things themselves, that causes our unhappiness or unhappiness.

Some recent trends in psychology support this ancient claim. In particular, contemporary Positive Psychology confirms the rightness of many aspects of the Greek view.[57] It considers that happiness is not something that merely happens to us, but, rather, a state of being which is comparable to physical health in that it must be actively pursued. In addition, Positive Psychology asserts that after a certain modest level of money has been attained, it is not relevant to happiness. This is because the wealthier one becomes, the more one seems concerned with measuring self-worth against the luxuries of the more affluent—and we always seem to find someone more affluent to compare ourselves to. Positive Psychology also believes that gratitude and forgiveness promote happiness. Finally, Positive Psychology invokes a largely cognitive strategy against depression insofar as it attempts to identify the thoughts that bring on unhappiness and to counter them rationally.

There is more than a slight affinity between Positive Psychology and Stoicism. Like Positive Psychology, Stoics assert that happiness is hard to achieve. Recall Marcus Aurelius on this point: "The art of life is more like the wrestler's art than the dancers."[58] So, not only for us, but for the Stoics as well, finding happiness requires sustained effort. Epictetus tells us that it is not possible to achieve the Stoic ideal of tranquility and equanimity "without great and constant practice,"[59] and he goes so far as to compare the work of internalizing Stoic principles to training in a gymnasium.

The Stoics go even further than Positive Psychology does in downplaying the role of material goods in a happy life, though both systems would see the energy most of us devote to our possessions as ludicrous. Rather than increase our happiness, the things we own end up burdening us. We buy a boat to go out on the weekends, and then have to work weekends to pay for it! "Since we are bound to many things," Epictetus laments, "we are depressed by them and dragged down."[60]

Forgiveness is an important concept in Stoicism, too. Like Positive Psychology, Stoics recognize the profound spiritual truth embedded in

Christ's counsel to love your enemies and to pray for those who persecute you: Negative emotions harm the possessor much more than they do those at whom they are directed. This is why the Stoics tell us to ignore the harm that others have done us. "Take away the opinion 'I have been harmed' and the complaint itself is taken away. Take away the complaint and the harm as well disappears."[61] There is no payoff in harboring anger and resentment towards others, for it merely disrupts our equanimity of spirit and undermines our peace of mind.

For similar reasons, gratitude is a state of mind that the Stoics also advise us to cultivate. It is an extremely economical emotion—just a little goes a long way towards providing us with a sense of well-being. Perhaps this is why one study cited by Positive Psychology concluded that quadriplegics have a higher level of life satisfaction than do lottery winners. It is therefore no surprise to find the Stoics advocating: "Think not so much of what you do not have as what you have. Select the best of these things, and then reflect how eagerly they would have been sought by you, if you did not already have them."[62] Finally, the Stoics would also have us follow the cognitive strategy recommended by Positive Psychology and be ever vigilant with regard to our thought process. "Such as are your habitual thoughts, such also will be the character of your mind," Marcus Aurelius informs us, "for the soul is dyed by its thoughts."[63]

If the number of years we live has now been extended, the parameters of the enterprise probably have not. We should therefore not be surprised to find that the insights of the Stoics are being resurrected some two thousand years after they were formulated, and that they are subsequently later being transformed into modern psychological principles. This, of course, diminishes neither Stoicism nor psychology, but rather reminds us of the timelessness of truth.

A Modern Day Stoic

Reports of Stoicism's demise have been greatly exaggerated. Probably no man has been more responsible for keeping the spirit of Stoicism alive in contemporary times than Dr. Albert Ellis. By applying Stoic principles to psychoanalytic method in the 1950's, he created a therapeutic method known today as Rational Emotive Behavior Therapy (REBT). He rejected the prevailing view that one needed to probe deeply into the unconscious in order to get to the source of an individual's problems, and asserted that our negative emotions are often the product of our own destructive beliefs. Since we ourselves are responsible for holding onto views that cause us to experience distress, we can change our emotional state by questioning the harmful, irrational beliefs we seem to be subject to, and replacing them with healthier, more rational ones. Dr. Ellis has been spreading this message for nearly half a century. His books have sold millions of copies, thousands of therapists have been trained in his method, and Dr. Ellis himself continues to see patients even though he is now in his eighties.

As he states in the classic work, *A Guide to Rational Living,* the key to REBT lies in understanding that many of our beliefs about ourselves are the result of internalized sentences—a sort of inner dialogue going on in our heads—and that often the things we tell ourselves are negative and self-defeating.[64] If we wish to change the destructive emotional states that result from this practice, we need first to recognize that we

Destructive Emotions   71

are guilty of this and then take steps to confront these harmful thoughts and replace them with healthier and more accurate assessments of ourselves. Consider, for example, the case of a woman who finds herself in a state of stress over an upcoming job interview.[65] She is probably engaging in a good deal of negative speculation, telling herself things like, "I'm a phony who is not qualified for this job," and, "I'm going to panic and blow this interview, then I'll be ruined." It is such thoughts—what Dr. Ellis refers to as Irrational Beliefs—that create the emotional stress. If the job candidate wishes to change her emotional reaction to the situation, she needs to alter her thoughts about the situation, providing herself with more positive messages such as, "I'm competent, I deserve this job, and if I don't get it, it's their loss." An interviewee who takes this attitude is much less likely to be stressed out (and therefore much more likely to get the job) than someone whose thoughts are driven by panic.

There is also the case of someone inadvertently stepping on one of our toes.[66] After we get over the initial pain, our natural reaction is to be angry at the person. When asked why we are so upset, we are likely to say something like, "Because that jerk stepped on my toe." But this is not entirely accurate. To be precise, the emotion is caused by our *thoughts* about the person who stepped on our foot, and can therefore be changed by altering those thoughts. Indeed, Dr. Ellis points out that our emotions are almost always sustained by ideas: "A large part of what we call emotion stems from a certain kind of thinking."[67]

These simple examples convey a fundamental point: Emotional reactions we often assume to be beyond our control are in fact caused by our own patterns of thought. Therefore, according to Dr. Ellis, reasoning with ourselves is, in fact, the key to unburdening ourselves of our unhealthy emotional states. Or, as he puts it, "If you would most thoroughly and permanently change your disturbed feelings, you'd better use considerable reasoning."[68] But, for us as moderns, the thesis that reason can lead us to a better emotional life sets our common assumptions on their head. We tend to believe that we simply find ourselves in certain emotional states, and that there is nothing we can do but learn to live with them. If we are happy, this is fortunate, and we hope the sensation lasts. If we are sad, we believe that our sadness is unavoidable, and we either wait for the feeling to subside or, in cases where it persists, we sometimes turn to anti-depressants. Indeed, the randomness of our emotions seems to be evidenced by the fact that they are often unrelated to external circumstances. We can be happy during the most un-

Chapter Two

fortunate events and depressed when all the details of our lives seem to be in exactly the right order.

In contrast to this, REBT argues that our emotions are for the most part within our control. A good example of the use of reason in dealing effectively with negative emotions can be seen in Dr. Ellis's discussion of one of the most commonly described psychological disturbances, namely, the sense of worthlessness.[69] If we have lost a job or ended a relationship, saying to ourselves something like, "This is a setback," is probably reasonable. Losing employment or companionship does, no doubt, interrupt our plans and will have some negative consequences for our lives, at least over short term periods, e.g., loneliness or depletion of financial resources. But realizing this amounts to making a reasoned assessment of the situation.

In spite our having the capacity for such rational thought, we can also find ourselves saying things like, "It is awful that I have failed at this task and this makes me a rotten person." Such a statement may have a negative impact on one's life, but it is, first and foremost, illogical. Awfulness implies a level of irreversibility and a set of adverse consequences having a magnitude that cannot reasonably or accurately be the case in this situation. Nor does the verdict that you are "a rotten, worthless person" have any basis in fact. It is a generalization that is based on an isolated incident. To think of oneself as worthless due to one or a few incidents would be as senseless as declaring that a racial group possessed a certain characteristic because one or two people who belong to it display this trait.

From this, we can conclude that it is the inability to rationally assess a situation (as opposed to the situation itself), that is responsible for our negative emotions. To counter this, we need to appraise the feelings logically, confront and expose the irrational beliefs that are causing them, and replace them with more rational ones. The notion that reason allows us to control our psychic health was no less radical than when it was proposed by Epictetus nearly two thousand years ago.

> These are not valid inferences. 'I am richer than you, therefore, I am superior to you' or 'I am more eloquent than you, therefore, I am superior to you.' But rather these are valid: 'I am richer than you, therefore, my property is superior to yours,' or 'I am more eloquent than you, therefore, my speaking ability is superior to yours.' But you are identical with neither your property nor with you speaking.[70]

Like REBT, Epictetus is here asserting that our emotions are caused by the things that we tell ourselves. In this instance, we are presented with someone who assumes that having significant wealth makes one superior and, by inference, lacking material goods makes one inferior. Epictetus challenges the logic of these thoughts, noting that the only valid inference that can be drawn from someone's having more material possessions than us is that the individual is wealthier than us. Finally, like Dr. Ellis, he seems to discard the illogical belief that our self-worth is tied to money and replace it with a healthier, more rational claim, namely, that we have inherent self worth ("you are identical with neither your property nor with your speaking").

Thus, ancient wisdom not only confirms the rightness of some modern thinking about the human person, but, in fact, it informs it. (Dr. Ellis makes no secret that he was influenced by the Stoics in general and Epictetus in particular.) Indeed, the web page for REBT includes the following quote: "What disturbs people's minds is not events but their judgments about events."[71] Of course, Dr. Ellis has done much more than merely parrot these ancient insights to the present generation. By integrating numerous traditions and applying his own genius, he has created a unique school of thought that has revolutionized the discipline of psychotherapy and improved the quality of countless lives.[72]

MISCELLANEOUS

MATTERS

The God of the Stoics

That Stoics should profess belief in the divine is hardly surprising. As Jung points out, it is only a handful of people over a short period of time on a small part of the Earth's surface that have taken it into their heads to dispose of the notion. Of course, the pervasiveness of the belief in God is not by itself relevant to the truth value of the proposition. Just because an opinion becomes firmly entrenched in a variety of cultures does not make it true. For thousands of years most people were convinced that the Earth was flat! But, the fact that a belief has been held for a long time doesn't necessarily mean it is false either. Prohibitions against killing are as old as humanity, and their soundness is generally not doubted.

Although those who believe in God are often connected to long-standing religious traditions, the various versions of the divine are and have been as multifarious as the people that inhabit this planet. It can therefore by no means be said that anything resembling a consensus has emerged on this question. Beyond the fact that they are regarded as transcendent forces, Allah, Yahweh, Vishnu ,and the Tao have precious little in common. So, if the Stoic position on God differs from more familiar ones, we should not be particularly surprised.

In mainstream Western theology, God is viewed as a specific being with particular characteristics, including omniscience, omnipotence and infinite goodness. Although humans possess degrees of these traits, God displays them to perfection. It is in part because we ascribe human

78   Chapter Three

properties to God that most picture Him as a wise, old man complete
with grey beard and flowing robes. This God tends to be construed in
two ways, either as the God of the Old Testament, a powerful being who
demands complete obedience and will use His fearful power to smite His
enemy, or as the loving God of the New Testament, who gave us His
only begotten Son so that we might be saved.

To understand the Stoic conception of God, it is necessary to completely step away from this anthropomorphic depiction and adopt a very
different view of the deity. Such a movement of thought is like making
a shift from the humanities to the hard sciences. The former covers
subjects like literature and history, and provides details of the lives of
interesting individuals and amazing events—both real and fictional—to
captivate and compel us: Captain Ahab and Napoleon, the Trojan War
and the Battle of Gettysburg. By contrast, the hard sciences range over
another type of subject matter, one replete with equations and laws,
abstract reasoning and deductive proofs. The Judeo-Christian God, as
He is understood today, might well be depicted as a God of the humanities, a fascinating figure with a great story to tell, while the Stoic God
could qualify as a God of the hard sciences, merely an abstract, organizing principle.

The Stoics accepted a version of what is known as the argument
from design, a mode of reasoning which dates back at least to Socrates
(through a report by Xenophon), although the most famous version of
which can be ascribed to the eighteenth century English theologian,
William Paley. If you are walking along the beach and find a watch in
the sand, he argues, you would not likely hypothesize that it had attained its particular configuration solely by chance. It is too intricately
designed, too obviously intended to carry out a specific purpose to be the
result of happenstance. It would make much more sense to infer that the
watch is a product of some talented craftsperson. Similarly, an examination of our physical surroundings—the varieties of plants and animals,
the ordering of the seasons, not to mention the wonder of human beings–ought to cause us to conclude that this world was likewise put
together by some creator, albeit one infinitely more intelligent than the
one who designed the watch.

Seneca is obviously using a version of this argument when he declares, "It is superfluous to point out that so mighty a structure does not
persist without some caretaker."[1] And just as the universe is obviously
the product of a rational mind, we too contain that same principle. For
the Stoics, that we can reason and think is no accident but a gift from
God. "You have a portion of Him in you," declares Epictetus. Our por-

Miscellaneous Matters

tion of the divine is reason: "The intelligence of every man is God, an emanation from the Deity."[2]

What is interesting about this conception of the divine is what both does and does not follow from it. There is no elaborate ritual or mass. There are no Stoic churches, no Stoic bible. The closest thing to a formal religious element in Stoicism may be the following from Marcus Aurelius: "The Athenians pray, 'Rain, rain, dear Zeus, upon the fields and plains of Athens'. Prayers should either not be offered at all, or else be as simple and ingenuous as this."[3]

And, perhaps most importantly, there is also no dogmatism in Stoicism. This is not a god you go to war over, or one in whose name you conquer and kill. If a person does not adhere to the Stoic conception of the deity, he is in error and suffers the consequences of believing something false—a state of being which brings with it its own burdens. People are not be persecuted for not believing 2+2=4, nor are mistaken beliefs about the divine to be condemned. Rather, the Stoic will merely point out the error, and this with the same equanimity as he would demonstrate in correcting a mathematical mistake: "You say they are mistaken," Marcus tells himself. "Why then, tell them so and explain it to them, instead of being indignant."[4]

There is, in Stoicism, also no doctrine of an afterlife or personal survival after death. Although this last claim may seem somewhat troubling to us, it need not. At his trial, Socrates declared that death was either a continued conversation or a long sleep, and that both situations were good. By way of explanation, he declared that there is nothing better than a dreamless night.

What does emerge from reflection on Stoicism's conception of a deity may, however, be somewhat surprising. Although God does not assure our eternal reward, nor smite our enemies, the universe He created does inspire awe and wonder. Gratitude is the quintessential Stoic religious emotion. Just as we can be grateful to our parents for bringing us into this world and providing for us, so the Stoic expresses gratitude to the Divine element that is ultimately responsible for our existence and has outfitted the earth, and ourselves, so lavishly. "Are you not willing," says Epictetus, "for so long as has been given you to be a spectator of His pageant and His festival, and then, when he leads you forth, to depart as a grateful and reverent spectator departs, to make room for others." And again, "For that Thou didst beget me I am grateful; for what Thou has given I am grateful also. The length of time for which I have had the use of Thy gifts is enough."[5]

However, not everyone can adopt such an attitude. The formality and ritual of traditional religion in the modern context in which we practice it can provide security, its claim of exclusivity can make us feel important, and its promise of reward can ease our fears. By contrast to this, the Stoic view resonates with those who feel a pure and simple wonder in the presence of the universe, and wish an avenue through which to acknowledge it—and nothing more.

When Bad Things Happen to Good Stoics

In *When Bad Things Happen To Good People*, Rabbi Harold Kushner confronts one of the oldest questions to plague humanity: How can an all-good and all-powerful God allow evil in the world, especially the evil that befalls the innocent? It would seem His power would give Him the ability to prevent any evil, and His goodness would require Him to do so. Yet, obviously, undeserved suffering afflicts endless numbers of innocent people (and others). Why? The Problem of Evil, as it is known in Judeo-Christian theology, has troubled the best minds throughout history, from the author of the Book of Job to Dostoevsky.

Examples of it are all too easy to document. A newspaper article reports that a man was sentenced to one hundred and twenty years in prison for sexual assault on a 9-year-old child, an attack that left the child blind, mute and crippled. Prosecutors said that the man lured the girl into an apartment at the crime ridden Cabrini-Green housing project in downtown Chicago, sexually assaulted her, poured roach spray down her throat, beat her and left her for dead in a dirty stairwell. Untold crimes no less heinous occur everywhere, everyday. Large scale atrocities such as the Holocaust or recent instances of ethnic cleansing are merely an extension of this same syndrome of sociopathic behavior. In light of all this, how can it be rational to believe in God?

There is no shortage of theodicies, or attempts to demonstrate that the existence of evil can be made consistent with an infinitely good and all-powerful Creator. One of the better known of these is referred to as

82 Chapter Three

"soul-making." It declares that the numerous difficulties that confront us in life exist in order to bring about our moral development. As one religious scholar put it, "A world in which no one can harm another, in which no pain or suffering results from any action, would not be a world in which moral and spiritual growth could occur."[6]

Such growth occurs in two ways, however. Not only do we ourselves spiritually mature as a result of confronting tragedy, but the reality of human suffering also provides a focus and a forum for others to progress morally, in so far as they attempt to combat it. On this view, God does not necessarily want us to have the most pleasant life, but rather wishes for us to develop as human beings over the course of our time on this planet. As the religious thinker C.S. Lewis put it, just like the blows of a sculptor on granite shape an unformed piece of material into something beautiful, so the pain and suffering in our lives can, if we allow it, transform us into something fully human.

Stoics, too, confront the problem of evil. Their conception of God may differ in numerous ways from the Judeo-Christian one, yet they still think of Him as creator and sustainer of the universe, and hence also claim that He bears some responsibility for the state of things. This is precisely why Seneca devotes an entire essay to the topic of "Why do many misfortunes fall to the lot of good men?"

Like the Judeo-Christian view, Stoics see the purpose of life as more than simply indulgence in pleasure: "To be lucky always and to pass through life without gnawing of the mind is to be ignorant of half of nature," argues Seneca. Rather than give this ease of passage "God hardens and scrutinizes and exercises those he approves of." Hence, we "should not shrink from hardship and difficulty or complain of fate; [we] should take whatever befalls in good part and turn it to advantage. The thing that matters is not what you bear but how you bear it."[7]

Marcus Aurelius is of the same sentiment: "Just as doctors prescribe horseback exercise, or cold baths, or going barefoot, so in the same way does the World Nature prescribe disease, mutilation, loss, or some other disability. In the former case, prescribing meant ordering a specific treatment in the interests of the patient's health; similarly in the latter, certain specific occurrences are ordered, in the interest of our destiny."[8]

In light of the fact that Stoicism exerted a tremendous influence on Christian ethical thinking, it should come as no surprise that both it and the Judeo-Christian tradition propose similar solutions to the problem of evil. Indeed, the view that the difficulties we encounter are a means to our development is probably one that would eventually be formulated by

Miscellaneous Matters

most any adept observer of the human condition. Certainly, anyone reading this volume has lived long enough to be able to cite similar examples or develop a similar theory, on the basis of his or her own experience.

There is, however, a problem here. Although we might admit that evil is necessary, in general, for our putting ourselves on a proper path to moral development, it is hard to see how this rule applies in some individual cases, or why some seem to have to suffer such great evils. Did the nine-year old girl in the story really have to be left mute, blind and crippled? Couldn't she have learned whatever it is she had to learn from undergoing maybe only two of the three types of injury? And what did she have to learn anyway? Did six million Jews and countless others *have to* perish in the Holocaust? Surely, whatever lessons people were to learn individually or collectively would not have been diminished had God struck Hitler dead after the first million Jews had been snuffed out.

In short, it seems impossible to make sense of the amount of evil in the world, or to find a lesson in every case. On this difficult point, the Book of Job is very instructive. Everyone is familiar with the story. Job, a pious man and faithful servant of the Lord, loses his children, his health and his property supposedly as a way of testing his faith. Despite the label that is sometimes attached to him, Job is, in fact, by no means patient about his situation but rails at God, demanding an answer to the question of why he, a good man, should suffer. His friends suggest he must have done something to deserve his fate, but Job proclaims his innocence and continues to press God for an explanation. Finally, near the end of the work, God appears as a voice from a whirlwind, not offering Job so much as an "I'm sorry" but instead simply flexing his muscle and telling Job that he has no right to inquire into such things. Oddly, Job is silenced by this behavior and simply declares, "I disown what I have said and repent in dust and ashes."

Not surprisingly, Biblical scholars disagree about the implication of Job's last statement. One plausible interpretation of it, however, is simply that he comes to recognize the limits of human understanding and realizes that some things must be resolved by faith. This notion—that the existence of evil defies ultimate explanation—strikes one as more humane than the hypothesis that evil is justified because it brings about moral development. It seems, for example, infinitely more compassionate to tell a woman whose child has died in a senseless car accident that "we don't know" why it happened rather than it is to declare to her that the event had some larger purpose, namely, to bring about her spiritual

84 Chapter Three

development.

Where do Stoics stand on the problem excessive evil? To begin, they deny that God has any explaining to do. Their reasoning is that since God gave all, he can justifiably take it all away. "Do you want the breath of my life?" asks Seneca. "Why not? I shall not balk at your taking back what you have given."[9] Similarly, Epictetus declares, "And so when you have received everything, and your very self, from another, do you yet blame the giver if he has taken something away from you?"[10] Gratitude characterizes the Stoic attitude towards misfortune, even excessive misfortune, more than complaining does. Quite simply, things happen that have no correlation to individual human desires, and the Stoic confronts what occurs with quiet resolve. "The business of a healthy eye is to see everything that is visible, not to demand no color but green, for that merely marks a disordered vision. In the same way, a healthy mind ought to be prepared for anything that may befall it. A mind crying 'O that my children be spared' is an eye craving for greenery."[11]

As noted earlier, the Stoics diverge from the Judeo-Christian explanation on the problem of evil. There are, however, significant parallels. Like the Stoics, Job concludes that God requires no explanation. And, by accepting the totality of what occurs with placid resolve, Stoicism approaches something akin to faith.

Was The Buddha a Stoic?

"For this is the origin of sorrow, to wish for something that does not come to pass."[12]

Students of Eastern philosophy will readily recognize the sentiment behind the above quote. In so far as the passage declares that the cause of suffering is related to unfulfilled desire, it embodies the spirit of the Second Noble Truth of Buddhism. But where exactly is the text found? These are the words of the Greek Stoic philosopher Epictetus, who lived more than 500 years later than the Buddha.

As will become apparent, this single sentence is not all these two philosophies–Stoicism and Buddhism–have in common. Indeed, the two systems are possessed of sufficient methodological and doctrinal likenesses such that one might legitimately wonder whether their similarities are mere coincidence. The intriguing, possible reasons for the parallels in thought patterns are not the topic to be explored here. Rather, the numerous doctrinal similarities between these two world views are what is of interest, as is the question of why these might matter to a practitioner of the Dharma.

Both Stoicism and Buddhism begin with the assumption that humans have a single goal: Happiness. The Stoics share with classical Greek thinking on ethics the belief in eudaimonism ('eudaimonia' is the Classical Greek word for happiness), the belief that the end of a rational agent is and ought to be his or her own happiness. That this sentiment should be paralleled in Buddhist thought is perhaps surprising, given

86   Chapter Three

the First Noble Truth of Buddhism:"Life is suffering." But while suffering is indeed the starting point for Buddhism, it is by no means the entirety of the story. The Buddha claims to teach not only the truth of suffering but also how it can be extinguished. Nirvana—the goal of Buddhism—is an end that may be achieved in this life. Both philosophies, then, are fundamentally practical in orientation, appealing first and foremost to people's desire to replace their current, unsatisfactory state of existence with a more fulfilling one.

In addition to sharing the same goal, the two systems of thought agree upon the biggest obstacle to this end. "For the origin of sorrow is this," says the Stoic philosopher Epictetus. "To wish for something that does not come to pass."[13] Likewise, according to the Second Noble Truth, in Buddhism the cause of suffering is desire. Our current state of unhappiness, then, is not a direct result of anything external but arises from our relationship with our own desires. The Buddha's prescription for our current state of misfortune is as famous as his diagnosis. If you wish to get rid of suffering, he states in the Third Noble Truth, you need to eradicate desire. At first glance, the Stoic attitude on this subject may seem radically different. For Epictetus informs us that he will reveal "how never to be disappointed" in what we desire.[14] Hence, it seems that one philosophy dismisses human longing as dangerous while the other guarantees its satisfaction.

Despite appearances, a deeper examination of these two systems reveals a remarkable convergence on this issue. In order to see this, we need to distinguish between two types of desire. Let me call desires that require elements outside of myself in order to be satisfied 'external' or 'object-oriented' desires, and those whose satisfaction relies on me 'internal' or 'state-oriented' desires. My longing for a new car, for example, would be an external desire since it requires elements beyond my control in order to be satisfied. For instance, I must have enough money, and the dealer must have the car in stock. By contrast, my wish to control my anger, or to be more generous to others, is completely up to me. If I fail to reach this goal, I have no one but myself to blame.

Buddhism, to be precise, does not tell us to abandon all desires. Rather, the Third Noble Truth should be interpreted as exhorting us to eliminate external desires, those whose satisfaction depends on factors beyond our control. This becomes clear when we reflect on the Eight-Fold Path that comprises the Buddha's prescription for how we ought to live: right view, right aspiration, right speech, right thought, right action, right livelihood, right mindfulness, right concentration. It seems

Miscellaneous Matters 87

reasonable to conclude that the Buddhist *does* have a desire to carry out these prescriptions, but it is also obvious that this qualifies as an 'internal' or 'state-oriented' desire whose satisfaction relies primarily on the individual. Right view, for example, calls on me to adopt a correct interpretation of the nature of reality, namely, one in line with the first three Noble Truths. As such, its attainment relies completely on my ability to achieve a correct cognitive state, and I can blame no one for my failure. Right aspiration asks me to engage with proper zeal upon the path, a factor that will likewise depend solely upon my level of motivation. Even the right actions that Buddhism dictates cannot, in any real sense, be frustrated. Short of being physically compelled, it is clearly up to me not to kill, steal, engage in sexual misconduct, lie or take intoxicants.

If the Buddhist claim to get rid of all desires is not as straight-forward as it might initially seem, Epictetus' boast that he will show us how never to have our desires thwarted is likewise an exaggeration. Clearly, there are some types of desire which Epictetus thinks we ought to toss out like bad milk. Hence, he informs us that striving after political power and wealth makes men abject and subservient to others. And as a rule, he says we should keep away from that which it is not in our power to acquire.[15] Indeed, the only desire Epictetus takes seriously is the individual's desire to retain equanimity. And, as he reminds us again and again, the satisfaction of this want is completely up to the individual.

In addition to sharing a goal (happiness) and a means (eliminating desires that do not depend on me and focusing on those that do), Stoicism and Buddhism utilize a similar methodology, one that differs radically from that which underlies other schools of thought in ethics. For most Western ethical systems, it is the action one engages in that determines an individual's moral worth. The Ten Commandments are perhaps the most famous example of a system that places the end of morality in activity (e.g., do not kill, honor thy father and mother). Most modern ethical theory takes the same tack, assigning moral praise based either on the consequences of my deeds (utilitarianism), or on whether they accord with some moral law (deontological ethics). By contrast, both Buddhism and Stoicism would claim that it is not the overt activity of an individual, but rather the mental state that precedes it, that is of primary ethical significance. In other words, moral intention is the primary issue for these thinkers. It is the mind's actions, not the body's, that become the standard by which the conduct is deter-

88 Chapter Three

mined to be ethical or not.

The primacy of the mental is evident from the very first words of the *Dhammapada*. "Mind is the forerunner of all actions," begins this classic Buddhist text. "All deeds are led by the mind, created by the mind. If one speaks or acts with a corrupt mind, suffering follows."[16] Since good thoughts are the foundation of ethics, we should direct our efforts at properly molding our intentions. "Just as an arrowsmith shapes an arrow to perfection with fire, so does the wise man shape his mind, for the mind, well-guarded and controlled, will bring happiness."[17] Similarly the emphasis in Stoicism falls on the proper state of the mind: "Nothing but judgement is responsible for the disturbance of peace of mind," says Epictetus.[18]

By way of explanation, the Stoic idea will claim that what upsets us is not that which is going on outside us, but rather, our reaction to events and circumstances. We see a luxury automobile, read about an exotic location, drive by a large house, or spot a particularly attractive person, and we are inwardly disturbed by our own reaction of envy. The cause of our distress, however, is not the fact that we lack that same type of material possession. Rather what upsets us is the judgment that the possession of these objects is necessary for our well-being. If we wish to be happy, we need to replace such defective judgments with healthier and more correct ones, for example, the insight that, beyond a certain minimal point, material goods have no relation to human happiness. In the spirit of the *Dhammapada*'s advice, the good Stoic fills his mind with such opinions. This is why Epictetus declares that "if you have sound judgments, you will fare well; if unsound judgments, ill."[19]

With such similar orientation, it is not surprising to find parallels between the *Dhammapada* and the *Meditations* of Marcus Aurelius. "Discard the thought of injury and the words 'I have been injured' are gone. Discard the words 'I have been injured' and the injury is gone" says Marcus.[20] "'He abused me, mistreated me, robbed me'. Harboring such thoughts keeps hatred alive. Releasing such thoughts banishes all hatred" echoes the *Dhammapda*.[21] The Buddhist classic states, "Pay no attention to harsh words uttered by others. Be not concerned with what others have done or have not done. Observe your own actions and inactions".[22] The Roman emperor replies, "How much ease he gains who does not look at what his neighbor says or does or thinks, but only at what he himself is doing in order that his own actions may be just, pious and good."[23]

If these sentiments sound familiar, it is perhaps because they have

Miscellaneous Matters 89

obvious parallels in the Gospels. Echoing the above passages, Christ enjoins us to ignore injustices and injuries done to us, and, instead, to love those who harm us. He likewise admonishes those who would focus on the misdeeds of others to "get rid of the beam in their own eye" before concerning themselves with the mote in their brother's. These are truly unusual passages in the Gospels and, along with the advice to seek poverty and not to resist evil, they are some of the least invoked in part because they seem to go against so much contemporary Christianity, which, unfortunately, seems to run contrary to Christ's own teachings in so far as its congregants often do not hesitate to judge others, to overlook Christ's endorsement of pacifism as a way of life, and to condone financial gain, even in the extreme. Buddhism and Stoicism, by contrast to this, do not hide such idiosyncratic claims but instead put them at the forefront of their moral systems.

Given the ideological affinities noted here, it is hardly surprising that both philosophies have been subject to remarkably similar criticisms. Historians of philosophy often charge Stoicism with being a philosophy of resignation, attractive only to those who have abandoned any hopes of seeing their plans in the world realized.[24] The Buddha's assertion that "life is suffering" is likewise often viewed as a pessimistic claim that entails a rejection of the world. It is certainly true that both systems advocate a certain detachment. "Altogether, human affairs must be regarded as ephemeral and of little worth,"[25] says the philosopher-emperor Marcus Aurelius. "Perceive the world as a bubble," counsels the *Dhammapada*. "Perceive the world as a mirage."[26] But this attitude towards the world is hardly unknown among great spiritual traditions, where there exists a recognition of a higher reality than the physical and a realization that this world of space and time is only worth taking so seriously. More importantly, it seems that a certain detachment from the world is not inconsistent with being engaged in it but is almost a prerequisite for such engagement, a buffer against the inevitable downturns and difficulties we confront in this life. Finally, as we have seen, the assertion that these philosophies are pessimistic is belied by the fact that they both claim happiness as their ultimate goal.

Far from recommending detachment, both philosophies stress action in and not withdrawal from the world. Mahayana Buddhism presents as an ideal the Bodhisattva, a being who has relinquished interest in his own salvation in order to work towards relieving the suffering of all sentient beings. Compassion, the Bodhisattva's preeminent virtue, propels one into the world and requires a commitment of time, energy and

90   Chapter Three

resources towards one's fellow beings. In much the same spirit, Stoicism stresses duty–something which does not seem so imbued with warmth as does the notion of compassion, but is equally as demanding in its requirements towards others. For example, Stoics adopted Aristotle's notion of man as a political animal, and required that adherents to their philosophy play their proper role in the affairs of state. In addition, Stoics were under a special obligation to their family, friends and relatives since nature herself had in one way or another established these roles. Finally, Stoics believed they had responsibilities to all creatures since humanity constitutes one giant brotherhood. "We are all fellow-citizens," says Marcus Aurelius, "and share a common citizenship, for the world is a single city."[27]

Given all of these similarities, it is still worth asking why one should bother to study Stoicism? Buddhism is the older of the philosophies, has a longer continuous history, and is much discussed in the West today. Why should we concern ourselves with a philosophy that has essentially lain dormant for more than fifteen hundred years?

It is doubtful whether one can ever have too many sources of inspiration. Since there have probably existed only so many first-rate minds and true spiritual masters, they are worth studying wherever they originate. The philosophy of Stoicism reveals that the West is not without its share of these, and their teachings may provide a different perspective and perhaps fresh insight for anyone seeking wisdom. Moreover, if indeed Stoicism does share some significant similarities to Buddhism, it may well provide an alternate pathway into certain truths that have seemed so attractive to many in the West. Demonstrating the parallels between Buddhism and Stoicism can be a useful mechanism through which to initiate students into Eastern thought, making an otherwise foreign and esoteric tradition seem much more inviting than might otherwise be the case.

Hence, both the experienced practitioner and the aspiring student of Buddhism have reason to undertake a study of this frequently neglected Western philosophy, and, given their spiritual predilections, they are probably much better situated than most of us to do so.

Satori and Stoicism

Walk into any gym in America and you will likely see signs touting the virtue of hard work, willpower and discipline. One poster at a facility I occasionally visit boldly declares that a workout is a combination of determination and perspiration, and even purports to give the proper percentage of each! The message "no gain without pain" is relayed in a dozen different ways here. Even the members themselves evidence the rewards that come from sticking with an exercise regimen and the danger that arises from neglecting the body for any length of time. Surely, in a society where instant gratification and easy credit are so frequently sought, where fad diets and get rich quick schemes are the order of the day, we cannot hear often enough the message that many important things in life require significant effort over a prolonged period of time.

When we turn to the spiritual realm, we might well expect what I will call "the logic of the gym" to apply. And, we might conclude following: Just as no one arrives at the height of physical achievement—the Olympics—without enormous and, to most of us, almost unimaginable preparation and sacrifice, so, too, one does not attain the pinnacle of the spiritual life, namely, enlightenment, without paying an equally high price. Both East and West are replete with stories of monks abandoning their secular lives and undertaking a regimen no less exacting than that of the highest trained athlete in order to realize their spiritual ideal.

Yet, we can also cite glaring counterexamples to this, cases where

92   Chapter Three

enlightenment was achieved in an instant, and sometimes without any effort. St. Paul's being struck down on the road to Damascus is perhaps the most famous example of this in the Christian West. But there are others as well. Secluded in a room after the death of Christ, the apostles were visited by the Holy Spirit and immediately infused with the ability to speak in tongues and accomplish great things. Even today, there are innumerable reports of similar conversion experiences. Those who undergo them often transform a lifetime of destructive behavior through the simple act of giving their lives to Christ.

Nowhere is this experience of instant enlightenment more evident than in the Zen Buddhist experience of satori. One always runs a risk in trying to explain anything about Zen Buddhism, a religion that likes to remind us that ultimate truth is beyond rational understanding. But the concept of satori is important enough that it is worth trying to say a few things about it. The great Zen scholar D.T. Suzuki asserts that without satori there is no Zen. According to Suzuki, satori involves, among other things, an entirely new and fresh perception of reality and an inevitable alteration of one's life.[28]

Since it is both the essence and the pinnacle of the lived experience of Zen, we would expect that satori might be experienced only after years of struggle and great sacrifice. Yet, extant tales tell precisely the opposite story. A young monk, Joshu, sought instruction in Zen. The master asked Joshu whether he had eaten breakfast. The young monk answered that he had, to which the master replied "Go and get your bowls washed." Immediately, Joshu's mind was opened and satori achieved. Another story tells of a novitiate receiving Enlightenment at the moment that a candle he is holding is blown out.

Such tales are meant to illustrate (but by no means explain) satori. There are endless stories of enlightenment occurring as the result of someone hearing an offhand comment, or a non sequitur. However, as was the case with St. Paul, the experience always involves a radical transformation of the subject, since it is an instantaneous movement from a state of being unenlightened to one of attaining wisdom and fulfillment. The fact that people have such experiences, does not, however, allow us to conclude that the spiritual life is easy and requires no effort. Rather, they remind us that the spirit or soul is something fundamentally different than the body, and the same laws do not always apply to both. The physical self could never attain its peak condition in an instant. But as the Bible reminds us, with the spirit, all things are possible.

Miscellaneous Matters 93

Given the universality of such experiences as these, we should not be surprised to discover that Stoicism, too, informs us that we can accomplish an extraordinary amount of spiritual progress in a remarkably short time. Marcus Aurelius states that "you have only to revert to the teachings of your creed, and to reverence for reason, and within a week those who now class you with beasts and monkeys will be calling you a god."[29] This is a pretty tall order, and it seems to be the spiritual equivalent of turning a 98-pound weakling into the beach bully in just seven days. But Marcus actually explains how this transformation can occur. It is not a matter of a magic pill or a new exercise machine, but a simple piece of reasoning. A number of character traits can be developed almost immediately should we wish to do so. What are they? "Sincerity, for example, and dignity; industriousness and sobriety." In addition we can "[a]void grumbling; be frugal, considerate, and frank; be temperate in manner and in speech; carry yourself with authority." He concludes: "See how many qualities there are which could be yours at this moment."[30]

Human spiritual life develops in response to some very fundamental longings. None seems more intractable than the desire to turn our lives around in an instant. Now that the bottom has dropped out of the stock market, any material aspirations that we may have (once again) require that we turn to thoughts of winning the lottery–at least most Americans would be inclined in this direction. It is easy enough to dismiss such fantasies. They are extraordinarily unlikely to happen, and even when they do, such an event is guaranteed to bring as much sorrow as joy. Such pipedreams are, however, as old as humankind–like the tale of finding a pot of gold at the end of the rainbow. In order to get at the their true meaning, we need to interpret these tales in a mythological fashion. If we do, then we realize that the 'gold' we are after is truly spiritual and, as St. Paul, Zen Buddhism, Marcus Aurelius and others remind us, it is nearer at hand than we realize.

Tuesdays with Marcus

At first, I thought I was the only one ever to engage in a certain practice, and so I kept it to myself, not exactly ashamed of it, but also not willing to announce it to the world. In time, however, I realized I was not alone. In the movie *Close Encounters of the Third Kind,* a number of people from all over the country find themselves mysteriously drawn to the same spot where aliens are about to land. Similarly, I ultimately discovered that something like a secret society existed of men and women like me who at some point in their lives and for a significant period of time have carried around a copy of *The Meditations* of Marcus Aurelius.

It's a highly recommendable practice. Sometimes the mere weight of the book next to your body is enough to provide a sort of grounding. More often than not, some particularly trying moment causes one to open the work at random—and discover surprisingly relevant words of wisdom.

Sometimes we're just looking for something to get us through the door, something which will give us some reason to go out into the world and take up the challenge again. At some point, we all ask ourselves why we're doing what we're doing—although our question is usually silenced by the routine of daily living—a routine that leaves us barely able to catch our breath, much less engage in any sort of existential analysis. The life circumstances of academics are, however, a little different. The several generous semester breaks that occur throughout

Miscellaneous Matters 95

the year make the grind more intermittent than constant, and there is indeed time (perhaps too much) to undertake such speculation. One feels especially vulnerable after a prolonged summer or Christmas break. Having adjusted to the fact of having no timetable, the commencement of classes is not unlike getting hauled out of a nice warm bed on a cold winter's morning. Since I was fortunate enough to have no classes the first day of the week, school for me began on a Tuesday one winter semester. At the start of classes on this particular January morning, I showered, dressed myself and ate, and found I had everything I needed to start another term–except motivation. Marcus Aurelius, what do you have to say about that? "Everything—a horse, a vine—is created for some duty. For what task, then were you yourself created? For pleasure? Can such a thought be tolerated?"[31]

That's what is so admirable about him! He doesn't pull any punches or tolerate any whining. We go to work for the same reason that we go to war—and for the same reason that we care for a sick child: Duty and obligation must, in the end, prevail. A citizen pays taxes. So, too, a member of the human community must contribute to the common good, and one of the ways to do this is by working. If we were to regularly ask ourselves where our duty lies instead of what our pleasure is, we might be in better shape. The paradox of hedonism states that the more we strive for pleasure, the less likely we will be to achieve it. Go out for an expensive meal, for example–treat yourself, and you are so aware you are supposed to be having a good time that it will be hard to get any actual enjoyment out of the experience. But, take a group of kids to some cheap pizza place for a birthday party because your wife told you to and you find yourself surprisingly delighted, despite the noise and inconvenience. At the end of the day, it will be the things we have to do, not the things we want to do, that will fulfill us.

To what insight does this reflection lead us? We ought to see our job as our calling (in the literal meaning of the term 'vocation'), something we have to do. Some extremes are, of course, to be avoided in this. On the one hand, there is not merely some single task we should be doing in order to experience enjoyment in life. Living with this expectation is a sure way to find ourselves quickly dissatisfied with our employment situation, since no real job can live up to any ideal we might fabricate, just as no real partner can satisfy someone in search of a movie screen fantasy. It is, however, also not the case that occupation is unimportant and that anything will do, so long as we are doing something to earn a living. One of the steps on the eight-fold path of Buddhism is called

96   Chapter Three

"right livelihood," or the notion that what we do is of importance in shaping us, and that it is inimical to our own well-being to work, for example, in an industry that degrades the human spirit or pollutes the environment.

So what are we to choose? Somewhere in between the thought "there is no job for my talent" and "it doesn't matter what I do" there lies the truth that there are a variety of occupations that will both utilize our unique skills and contribute to the public good. Marcus Aurelius would say: "Give your life to the trade you have learned, and draw refreshment from it."[32]

Since the Aurelius volume looks awkward sticking out of my back pocket, I usually don't carry it into class. One day, however, perhaps because it was the first day of the semester, I slipped up—a fact for which I would soon be grateful. When I walked into class, one student stood out immediately—he wast asleep at his desk! Rather than get angry I reached for my copy of the *Meditations*. "Everything that happens is as natural and expected as the spring rose or the summer fruit."[33]

Recently, a Marx Brothers' movie was playing. It was the one in which Groucho plays the newly appointed president of a university. The first decision he must make concerns whether to build a new football stadium, or more dormitories. He opts for the former. Where, he is asked, will the students sleep? "Where they always sleep," he replies. "In the classroom." Is this movie perhaps not already seventy years old? Should I have expected things to change? Troubles with students have plagued philosophers for centuries. Nietzsche had difficulty attracting students and would often find himself lecturing to no more than a few, while St. Augustine quit teaching in Rome because he could not make himself heard over the clamor of those attending class. If these men could put up with all of this, then perhaps a modern American professor ought also to tolerate a snoring student with humor and dignity. ("Hey, you're not supposed to fall asleep until after I start lecturing.")

It's good to get outside and all too easy to have the day pass by only to realize at the end of it that you should have ventured more than a few hundred feet from your office. But, even starting the stroll across campus is almost enough to make one regret a decision to go out. It's cold, damned cold. The more one walks, the more depressed one gets. There is nothing but signs of a prolonged winter. Deep snow, barren trees, and an ominous sky. Great for the skiers. And the air gets dirty, trapped by an unpleasant and unhealthy meteorological phenomenon known as an

Miscellaneous Matters

inversion. Well Marcus? "Loss is nothing else but change, and change is Nature's delight. Ever since the world began, things have been ordered by her decree in the selfsame fashion as they are this day, and as other similar things will be ordered to the end of time. How, then, can you say that anything is amiss?"[34]

In this spot on midsummer afternoons, the sun was beating down at a hundred degrees; on crisp, cool autumn days, the mountains were blanketed not in snow but with the changing colors of the leaves. The warmth of the spring winds has brought out the first buds on the trees, and the sun has often peeked over the mountains in the morning as I trundled across campus. On this spot, too, these same mountains have been lit by the setting sun as if in a raging blaze. Truth be told, seeing all of this has been good—eeven the moments of chill and unpleasantness—if I'm willing to open myself up to the larger experience and realize, with Marcus, that it's all part of a cyclical process. The snow, wind, clouds and haze all are to be thanked for reminding one of all this.

At the end of the day, it is a good practice to examine one's spiritual balance sheet—and hopefully find that the pluses outweigh the minuses. That's not always the case, and more than a few times I have found myself facing a significant spiritual deficit. At such moments, the desire to throw in the towel is overwhelming. Instead, I pick up the book: "Manifestly no condition of life could be so well adapted for the practice of philosophy as that in which chance finds you today."[35]

Very often, we want to return to an earlier period of life, when things seemed happy and carefree, or, alternatively, flee to a later time, when the troubles one is facing will have subsided. But Marcus reminds us that everything we need for salvation is right here in the present—a particularly fortunate fact, given that the present is all we ever really have. What better place to start from than that of spiritual imperfection. Someone who is just getting into shape may have a long way to go before she can run a marathon, but she is also going to see vast improvements in her condition with relatively little effort. A mile or so a day will do it. We are not asked to be Stoic sages or Zen masters, but simply to work on ourselves and to take that project seriously. That may be enough for now.

Practice, Practice, Practice

"So, are you a Stoic?"

The question inevitably arises whenever I present these essays to an audience, lecture on Stoicism to a class, or discuss my ideas with friends and acquaintances. It is not an easy question to answer, although it is a fair one to ask. A person espouses a set of doctrines and you naturally enough want to know his relation to them. Is he serious about what he is professing? And, if he's not, why should we be?

The question poses a very old problem—one that goes back at least to Socrates. If you are going to say whether something is an 'x', you first have to define what 'x' is—something that is not, as Socrates' followers discovered, an easy task. We want our social institutions to be just, but what is 'justice'? So in order to classify someone as a Stoic, one must, therefore, have a clear definition of a Stoic. If one accepts Christ as savior, takes the sacraments, accepts the Bible as the word of God, and attends church regularly, that suffices to qualify one as a Christian. Stoicism, however, has no such litmus test, no set of clearly defined standards or formalized system of obligations. Nonetheless, there may be some general guidelines which can be said to characterize it.

Being a Stoic requires that one take a certain stance toward life, in particular towards (I) one's desires, (II) society and circumstances, and (III) the universe.

I. Desires

Perhaps the most revolutionary of the Stoic insights concerns the nature of desire and our ability to conquer it. We are raised to think that the more desires we have, and the better able we are to fulfill them, the happier we will be. Yet, ironically, in a land like America, where more people can satisfy more of their desires than at any place or time in human history, unhappiness is widespread and the use of anti-depressants is at an all time high. What has gone wrong? Not surprisingly, the Stoics inform us that the problem has to do with desire. We long for things we can't possibly attain, things that can readily be taken away from us, or things that, by their nature, can't and won't bring happiness. In short, we search for our own well-being in people, places, and objects which are outside of ourselves and, ultimately, beyond our control. If, however, true happiness is what we are wishing for, the Stoics tell us we should instead focus on something internal—something we can control, namely, the ability to keep our peace of mind no matter what happens. Satisfying this desire is always up to us, given the proper practice, and hence, so is happiness.

II. Society and Circumstances:

We want events to unfold in accord with our plans. Similarly, we wish friends, family, colleagues and even strangers to conform to our expectations. Of course, virtually none of this happens. Yet, surprisingly, we become upset. As a way to deal effectively with the many contingencies of life, Stoicism adopts a creed that might at first seem fantastic or almost delusional: Act as if you had actually willed whatever it is that has happened. Although this is a stance which is initially difficult to achieve, adopting it allows us to benefit from whatever occurs and to greet all events with the equanimity we truly desire. How can one get upset at what one has desired to take place?

Likewise with regard to human interaction, we need to acquire a new attitude if we wish to attain peace of mind. We must assume a level of determinism is operative in everyday life, and convince ourselves that men and women behave as they do because of who they are and what they have previously experienced. Recognizing that they can't help but do what they do goes a long way towards establishing harmonious relations with others and hence, also, maintaining our own psychic balance.

III. Universe

Finally, in order to achieve any sort of lasting peace, we need to attain a satisfying view of our relation to the whole of creation. Concerning this this, Stoics suggest first that we assume that, on some level, fate is working itself out in our lives. Accepting the inevitability of whatever happens allows us to relax rather than try to control events. Stoics also ask us to realize (again for the sake of our tranquility), that we are but a very tiny part of the universe. Attempting to view events from the perspective of the larger, uncreated order, can likewise have a very calming effect on us.

As Epictetus reminds us, "if we do not refer to some standard, we shall be acting at random."[36] Stoics not only accept this as a worthy ideal, but they also make a concerted effort to adopt such insights as the organizing principles of their existence. Epictetus stressed that being a Stoic consists essentially of subjecting oneself to such discipline and practice. "A bull is not made suddenly, nor a brave man . . . we must discipline ourselves for a winter campaign."[37] In other words, it seems there are three things required to become a Stoic: practice, practice, and more practice.

Do I Contradict Myself?

Unfortunately, the previous essay doesn't answer the question it posed initially: "Am I a Stoic?" That it did not was no accident. Labels have always seemed stultifying—for myself or anyone else. To paraphrase Emerson, if I know your creed, I can anticipate beforehand what you are going to say.

Furthermore, labels seem to separate human beings from one another. If we subscribe to one or another school of thought because we feel it gets at the truth about existence, then we invariably set ourselves up as superior to those who have taken on other labels: We are correct, so they must be mistaken! Labels also allow us to reduce others to mere adherents of certain doctrines instead of seeing them as people. They thereby make it a lot easier to dismiss them and even harm them. The Middle East is close to imploding, due in no small part to the power of the labels "Muslim" and "Jew." Finally, adopting one doctrine as the organizing principle of our existence and dubbing ourselves followers of a given figure seems to give rise to a tendency to recruit others to our side. I may be overly sensitive to this issue because I live in Utah, where proselytizing is a way of life, and I see the divisions this creates.

Even the appellation "Stoic" is one which ought, therefore, to be applied with caution. Epictetus expressed concern about this: "When you intend to exercise yourself for your own advantage, and you are thirsty from the heat, take in a mouthful of cold water and spit it out and tell nobody."[38] Christ gave the same advice when he told people

102   Chapter Three

who wish to pray to shut themselves in their room and not to make a public display of it. Unfortunately, this plea for discretion is routinely ignored–a fact which is sufficiently illustrated by the phenomenon of televangelists. Politicians also often conveniently publicize their faith in an effort to prove their moral probity, often when their actions seem particularly disreputable. Over against all of this, Epictetus' advice echoes in our ears: "Practice first not to let men know who you are; keep your philosophy to yourself a little while."[39]

But, attaching labels to people and schools of thought seems to be a necessary part of life, so the question posed at the start of the previous essay is not easily evaded. Still, it presents a real dilemma. If we refuse the title "Stoic," we risk having our sincerity called into question for espousing a philosophy we are not actually willing to claim adherence to. If, on the other hand, we adopt the appellation, do we not merely increase the numbers of labels that already exist in the world, and thereby add to divisiveness that they already create? Some sort of response is indeed in order here.

The old sitcom, *The Odd Couple*, is about two divorced men living together, one who is a neat freak, the other an inveterate slob. One particular episode shows roommates Felix and Oscar going through a mid-life crisis together after they have encountered a group of younger people. Having concluded that their own lives have become too staid and predictable, they decide to shake things up by changing their clothes, altering their hairstyles and joining their new friends in a variety of adventures in alternative culture. All goes well until one evening when they have planned to meet their companions at two o'clock in the morning for a psychedelic bus trip. In the final scene, Felix is sitting by Oscar's bed, discussing how foolishly they've been acting lately, and how they need to accept their age with dignity, letting go, as the Bible says, of the things of one's childhood. When Oscar asks Felix whether he has awakened him just to lecture him on this, Felix says, "No, it's almost two a.m.–time to get up and get ready to catch the bus." In a similar spirit, Whitman proclaimed: "Do I contradict myself? Very well then, I contradict myself. I am large; I contain multitudes." Hence, I conclude we should accept the label "Stoic" only if we can in good conscience violate every one of its major tenets from time to time!

Such a requirement that we allow ourselves to be inconsistent might, at first, seem inimical to our hope of living any sort of meaningful moral life. Generally, we call people who ardently espouse one principle, then act in such a way as to violate it "hypocrites." In reality,

Miscellaneous Matters

however, the ability to accept something less than perfection from both ourselves and others seems a necessary step to the process of becoming fully human. What are we, really, but good Christians who haven't given everything to the poor and don't always turn the other cheek; environmentalists who own an SUV; feminists who like to have the door held open for them; vegetarians who sneak a cheeseburger now and then; fundamentalists who occasionally check out an Internet porn site; Republicans who favor social spending; Democrats who wouldn't mind a tax cut, et cetera. In other words, do we not all try to do the best we can, but, more than occasionally, make a mess of things?

The opposite of this, the belief that we must rigidly adhere to a strict standard of behavior and make no room for exceptions seems to be the beginning of fanaticism, rather than an admirable scheme of personal discipline. It also tends to distance us from others and even alienate us from ourselves. If we succeed in adhering to our ideals consistently and without exception, we begin to perceive as weak those who fall short of what we believe to be the level of moral perfection we have attained. If, on the other hand, we fail to live up to a self-imposed standard, we defeat ourselves before we can even seriously set out on the path of moral development. Either way, it's a losing proposition.

As noted earlier, a Stoic should generally keep below the radar screen, both for his own good and for that of others. This is why the label "Stoic" can only tentatively be accepted—for the time being, and in the recognition that, at the end of the day, not much hangs on any particular title. Is this not a somewhat tepid endorsement of Stoicism? Perhaps, but downplaying the role of labels is not inconsistent with adopting a goal or ideal as a guide. Doing so merely amounts to recognizing that ideology is largely a matter of indifference, that the labels we do accept are taken up as a result of circumstances, and that, as a rule, people are trying to do the best they can with their lives.

This is not to suggest that Stoicism ought not to be taken seriously. But truth be told, we don't take ourselves all that seriously. In his last great work, *The Laws*, Plato says we should recognize that we are playthings of the gods and act accordingly. Such a remark may be misinterpreted as endorsing moral laziness, but the notion that we are the gods' playthings emphasizes the reality that the majority of events in life are ultimately beyond of our control, and that, despite our best efforts, we will have but little impact on the world—and even that will be erased over time. A little sympathy for our fellow humans and even ourselves therefore seems called for: A willingness to accept imperfection and inconsistency, to live with each other's—and our own—foibles, and, finally, to laugh, as Seneca said, rather than cry at life.

Be Prepared

There's a Woody Allen short story about a man who, disenchanted with reality, invents a machine to put himself into the plots of novels. A fan of Flaubert, he inserts himself into his favorite book, *Madam Bovary*. All over the country, teachers of literature are surprised to find a balding, middle-aged Jewish man having an affair with Emma Bovary. One professor even comments on how this only demonstrates that we can always find something new when we re-read a great book.

Even if one has often pored over the Stoic texts, some things still jump out at one as if for the first time. A thought, a sentiment, or an observation can seem so profound that it couldn't possibly have been missed on an earlier reading. Maybe some Woody Allen-like character has injected, not himself, but his thoughts into works of philosophy?

Recently when leafing through the pocket-sized volume of Marcus Aurelius' *Meditations* mentioned earlier, I read the following: "How ludicrous and outlandish is astonishment at anything that happens in life."[40] I could only put down the book, shake my head and think, "How true." What event on this earth should catch us off guard? Yet, we act surprised at many things. We often can't believe we're stuck in traffic, that our car has broken down, that we had a bad day at work, that a check bounced, that a friend lied, or that a lover cheated, et cetera. And then there are the big three, the ones that struck the young Buddha as he snuck out of the city in search of a different form of life: old age, sickness and death. Who cannot see those coming?

106   Chapter Three

In such situations, it is because some wish or hope of ours is not fulfilled that we feel some mental disturbance. We assume our car will get us to work and are upset to come out in the morning and find that it won't start. We schedule our day believing we will be healthy, and are irritated when we get sick. In certain respects, our expectations are reasonable. Cars work most of the time, and we're healthy more often than not. But, as everyone knows and the famous saying reminds us, "stuff happens." To be disturbed by any inconvenience, setback or disappointment in life is, therefore, a bit like living in Seattle and being put off when it rains. Such a reaction is simply not the act of a rational agent.

The Stoics had a particular way of dealing with this phenomenon, one which many today may find helpful. "When you are about to undertake some action, remind yourself what sort of action it is. If you are going out for a bath, put before your mind what happens at baths—there are people who splash, people who jostle, people who are insulting, people who steal."[41] In other words, if we see something coming our way, we are much less likely to get upset if we can actively anticipate it than if we cannot. An expected insurance bill does not move us to rail at the universe the way a tax lien from out of the blue might. A vaccine innoculates by introducing a small dose of the disease; so, too, if we prepare ourselves ahead of time for events we're likely to encounter at a given point by bringing them before our mind, we will be better able to maintain a degree of equanimity when such events do occur.

Beginning with little things is advisable if we are going to practice this well. If we are going to the grocery store, then we need to remind ourselves ahead of time of the things that can happen. The store might be low on (or out of) certain items, it might be crowded, and someone in the express lane might have lost the ability to count. If we prepare ourselves in advance, when these circumstances occur, we can calmly tell ourselves that such things are to be expected. It is within our power to treat daily events in the same manner. You are commuting to work. Is a traffic jam which develops while we are on the way to work such a shock? Or, is it not just one of the things that happens on highways? Suppose a child gets sick? Well, they do that sometimes. It is simply not the mark of a rational persons to be upset by the inevitable, the predictable, the all too human.

Epictetus would have us undertake such a process on a daily basis. "As soon as you get up in the morning bethink you 'what do I lack in order to achieve tranquility'? What are the demands upon you? Re-

Miscellaneous Matters

hearse your actions."[42] Such a suggestion (and it seems a sound one) directs us to take a little quiet time each morning to reflect on what lies ahead, in both the short and long term.

For teachers, everyday life inevitably brings inattentive students, recalcitrant colleagues, indifferent administrators, lesson plans that don't work, meetings that go on too long, et cetera. But, of these things and the others we experience, what exactly lies within our control? To do our jobs as best as possible and remain calm. Reminding ourselves of this, both at the start of the day as well as over the course of it, can lead to a lot fewer surprises and less irritation.

Epictetus would, however, have us bring to mind even starker realities: "Let death and exile and everything terrible appear before your eyes every day, especially death."[43] This may sound morbid, but actually it is not. As noted elsewhere, the point of this exercise is that, as the song says, we often don't know what we got till it's gone. To contemplate the loss of our health, our friends, our family and finally our own life can truly help us to appreciate what we *do* have at present.

But, are the Stoics recommending a sort of sky-is-falling mentality? No, they aren't. Nor would they have us go through everyday life waiting for the worst to happen. To accuse them of emphasizing the negative aspects of our existence is to misinterpret them—to misunderstand what exactly they are asking of us. They are not suggesting that we ought to walk under a black cloud all day, so to speak, but rather that a little mindfulness—mentally rehearsing actions before carrying them out—can aid us and perhaps prevent mishaps. The reason to focus on possible negative or problematic events is that we don't really need to prepare for the good things—they don't derail us. Nor is it correct to assert that preparing for bad things in the way the Stoics would have us do is a way of inviting the universe to make them happen. The belief that we exercise that sort of control over the nature of things borders on megalomania.

The goal is, as Boy Scouts have long known, ultimately a very simple one: Be prepared.

Three Years

As I write this, the New Year is approaching. People are preparing resolutions and getting ready to put their old, stale lives behind them. There are pounds to be lost, training programs to be implemented, languages and musical instruments to be mastered, far away lands to be visited, faults to be remedied. At the darkest time of the year, when the days are oppressively short and the nights seemingly endless, we manage to convince ourselves that we can wipe the slate clean and start anew.

In and of itself, there is nothing wrong with this. There may even be something noble about such a flood of optimism. Rebirth and regeneration are themes as old as humanity. Without the prospect of renewal, life would become one sad event after another–a single mistake would doom us forever. Indeed, it is the feeling of being beyond such redemption that often impels people to suicide. The problem lies, however, not in our aspirations, but in what happens afterwards. Within a couple of weeks, if not sooner, ninety-five percent of all these well-intentioned plans will have fallen through, and we will be right back to where we started.

As the Stoics see it, part of the difficulty lies in *what we hope for*. We would become better persons, we tell ourselves, but we very often choose some very odd ways of achieving that end. Losing a few pounds, for example, has about as much to do with true improvement as digging a ditch does with learning German. Indeed, if we examine any list of

Miscellaneous Matters 109

New Year's resolutions, it will invariably be composed of items that Stoics see as having no inherent value. The fitness of our body, for example, is not something we have any final control over–disease and sickness can come despite our best intentions and efforts. Financial well-being can also be undermined regardless of how much we save or plan. According to the Stoics, nothing that can be taken from us against our will ought to be an ultimate object of pursuit. Although there is not anything wrong with being in physical shape or getting our financial affairs in order, to put such goals at the top of our resolution list, as we invariably do, evidences perhaps too much of a concern for what is truly unimportant. As the Bible reminds, we cannot serve two masters.

But more important than what we hope for is *the way we hope for it.* The problem here—as many have pointed out—is that our society has become a culture of instant gratification. We expect our Big Mac within a minute after placing the order, or we are upset. We demand of a retailer that the big screen television be set up and functioning in our homes the day after we saw it at the store, or we threaten to purchase it elsewhere. With the advent of the internet and overnight mail, there is no product we cannot acquire almost the instant we wish for it. So, we adopt the same attitude towards a slimmer body or musical proficiency and become dismayed and discouraged when we realize that tremendous effort and long stretches of time are required for even minimal progress in these things.

The flip side of this is that once our inflated hopes become dashed against the shores of reality, our attitude toward any possible change tends to become one of cynicism. Abandoning ourselves to forces of inertia, we shake our heads at those in search of transformation and resign ourselves to the lifelong companionship of our shortcomings and failures. If love can all too easily turn to hate, so, too, can naive New Year's optimism quickly be reduced to despair, or worse, to a sort of entrenched resignation in the face of the unsatisfactory condition of our souls.

There exists, however, another path to effectively dealing with ourselves–one that is to be found between the extremes of unrealistic expectation and sorrowful surrender. Marcus Aurelius chides himself: "Even at this late hour, set yourself to become a simpler and better man in the sight of the gods. For the mastering of that lesson, three years are as good as a hundred."[44] Three years. That sounds just about right. Few of us–not even the recently diagnosed cancer patient—do not hope to have that period of time remaining. So the project has a universal di-

110   Chapter Three

mension, since we can all expect to achieve at least some degree of completion. Moreover, such a period of time is long enough to get us beyond the idea that the desired transformation is going to occur instantly, but, yet, short enough not to allow us to put things off indefinitely. One of the problems with New Year's resolutions is that they implicitly carry with them the notion that they will be followed for the rest of our lives. No one desires to lose weight and then get it back again in six months, or to build a nest egg only to quickly deplete it. But it is precisely the indefinite time frame involved in such plans that facilitates backsliding. If we know we are going to have to stand watch both day and night for a week, it is likely that our attention will wane, whereas if it is only for a few hours, we will probably remain much more in tune with our surroundings for the duration of our watch. The goal of three years—thirty-six months—therefore allows us to keep our sights focused on the relatively near future and not lose a sense of urgency about the undertaking.

This time period also allows one to confront the not uncommon feeling of stagnation that can overcome one, especially at middle age (although it can certainly occur at other times, too), a sense that there is no point in attempting to improve ourselves because it is much too late in the game. Not so, says Marcus Aurelius. He assures us that an ample number of days is still allotted to us so that we may, once and for all, get our affairs in order. Any denial that this is possible amounts to mere laziness. Finally, if we keep in mind the three-year time frame, we will also be able to avoid the notion that with one bold, usually foolish, move we can erase all the errors of the past and begin anew.

The Roman emperor's resolution list is short: To become a simpler and better man in the sight of the gods. Here, we recognize the Stoic dictum, namely, to concern ourselves only with what is within our control. Nor should it be surprising to find that it is only by working on such things that true transformation can occur anyway. Seneca reminds us that "for a happy existence one needs only a sound and upright soul, one that despises fortune."[45] Of course there is a problem here. We can't join a health club in order to become simpler and better persons, nor is there any class we can take to achieve a sound and upright soul. Still, the same principle applies on both the spiritual and the physical levels. We need to devote a certain amount of time and energy to the task in order to accomplish anything.

If we are really serious about spiritual self-improvement, then we will discover that there are certain time-tested ways of proceeding:

Miscellaneous Matters 111

Reading the spiritual classics, setting aside a certain amount of time for meditation and reflection, keeping a journal, engaging in service to others, et cetera. These are all good starting points, but, at the end of the day, every individual's path to progress in this realm will be his or her own.

Perhaps the best piece of advice on this comes from the American Stoic, Henry David Thoreau. In a parable from *Walden,* he depicts the plight of an Everyman contemplating his own life and the possibility of change:

> A voice said to him,—Why do you stay here and live this mean, moiling life, when a glorious existence is possible for you? Those same stars twinkle over other fields than these.—But how to come out of his condition and actually migrate thither? All that he could think of was to practice some new austerity, to let his mind descend into his body and redeem it, and treat himself with ever increasing respect.[46]

Happy New Year!

Notes

Introduction: Stoicism: The Path to Personal Liberation

1. Epictetus, *Discourses*, translated by W.A. Oldfather (Cambridge, Massachusetts: Harvard University Press, 1925), 3.24.18.
2. Epictetus, *Enchiridion*, translated by W.A. Oldfather (Cambridge, Massachusetts: Harvard University Press, 1925), 1.
3. *Ibid.*
4. Marcus Aurelius, *Meditations*, translated by George Long, 7.68.
5. *Discourses*, 3.13.11.
6. *Meditations*, 2.5.
7. Seneca, "On Tranquility," in *The Stoic Philosophy of Seneca*, translated by Moses Hadas (New York: W.W. Norton,1958), p. 80.
8. *Discourses*, 4.10.22.
9. See, for example, *Discourses* 1.4, 1.24, 2.17, 2.18, 3.15, 3.25, 4.8.
10. *Discourses*, 1.2.32.
11. Seneca, "Consolation to Helvia," in Hadas, p. 111.
12. *Discourses*, 4.7.12.
13. *Meditations*, 3.5.
14. Seneca, *Letters from a Stoic*, translated by Robin Campbell (New York: Penguin, 1969) p. 64.
15. *Ibid.*

Part I: Difficulties and Disappointments

1. Epictetus, *Enchiridion*, 3.
2. *Enchiridion*, 1.
3. Seneca, "On Tranquility," in Hadas, p. 91.
4. *Ibid.*
5. Seneca, "Consolation to Helvia," in Hadas, p. 120.
6. Seneca, *Letters from a Stoic*, p. 75.
7. *Ibid.*, p. 190.
8. Marcus Aurelius, *Meditations*, 11.18.
9. *Ibid.*
10. *Ibid.*
11. *Ibid.*
12. *Enchiridion*, 28.
13. Epictetus, *Discourses*, 3.2.4

114 Notes

14. *Enchiridion*, 3.
15. *Enchiridion*, 21.
16. *Meditations*, 7.69.
17. Seneca, *On Providence*, in Hadas, p. 42.
18. *Discourses*, 4.10.27.
19. *Meditations*, 5.29.
20. *Meditations* 7.56.
21. *Letters from a Stoic*, p. 73.
22. *Ibid.*, p. 44.
23. Carl Jung, *The Portable Jung*, (New York: Viking, 1971), 17.
24. *Meditations*, 9.41.
25. *Ibid.*
26. For an example of the Stoic view of indifferents see, for example, *Discourses*, 3.20.4.
27. *Enchiridion*, 44.
28. *Discourses*, 3.10.12.
29. *Ibid.*

Part II: Destructive Emotions
1. Epictetus, *Enchiridion*, 8.
2. Epictetus, *Discourses*, 3.10.19.
3. *Enchiridion*, 43.
4. *Discourses* 1.24.2.
5. *Ibid.*, 1.4.23.
6. Victor Frankl, *Man's Search for Meaning*, (New York: Washington Square Press, 1959).
7. Marcus Aurelius, *Meditations*, 4.49.
8. His Holiness The Dalai Lama and Howard C. Cutler, *The Art of Happiness: A Handbook for Living*, (New York: Putnam Publishing Group, 1998).
9. *Meditations*, 12.4.
10. *Discourses*, 1.9.
11. *Meditations*, 7.9.
12. *Discourses*, 1.3.1.
13. *Meditations*, 5.24
14. *Ibid.*, 6.36.
15. *Ibid.*
16. *New American Bible*, Jean Marie Heisberger, General Editor (Oxford: Oxford University Press, 1995), p. 782.
17. *Meditations*, 9.32.
18. *Enchiridion*, 3.
19. *Ibid.*, 11.
20. *Ibid.*, 16.
21. *Discourses*, 3.24.5.

Notes   115

22. *Ibid.*, 3.24.60.
23. *Ibid.*, 3.24.34.
24. *Ibid.*, 2.16.32.
25. *Enchiridion*, 16.
26. *Discourses*, 2.13.7
27. *Ibid.*, 2.16.45.
28. *Ibid.*, 3.13.11.
29. Daniel Goleman, *Emotional Intelligence* (New York: Bantam, 1995), p.46.
30. *Discourses*, 2.18.25.
31. *Discourses*, 2.16.22.
32. *Meditations*, 3.13.
33. *Meditations*, 9.42.
34. *Meditations*, 11.18.
35. *Ibid.*
36. *Discourses*, 4.3.7.
37. Goleman, p. 56.
38. *Ibid.*, p. 62.
39. *Meditations*, 11.18.
40. *Ibid.*
41. Goleman, p. 65.
42. Seneca, *Consolation to Helvia*, 10.
43. Goleman, p. 69.
44. *Ibid.*, p. 74.
45. *Enchiridion*, 43.
46. *Discourses*, 1.12.21.
47. *Ibid.*, 3.20.12.
48. Goleman, p. 86-88.
49. *Meditations*, 4.17.
50. Seneca, *Letters from a Stoic*, p. 64.
51. Goleman, p. 96-110.
52. *Discourses*, 1.13.4.
53. *Meditations*, 4.4.
54. *Discourses*, 2.10.4.
55. *Ibid.*, 2.23.38.
56. Aristotle, *Nichomachean Ethics*, i.4.
57. "Psychology discovers happiness," by Gregg Easterbrook in *The New Republic* 3/15/01, 20-23.
58. *Meditations*, 7.61.
59. *Discourses*, 3.12.5.
60. *Ibid.*, 4.1.
61. *Meditations*, 4.7.
62. *Ibid.*, 7.27.
63. *Ibid.*, 5.16.

116 Notes

64. Albert Ellis, *A Guide to Rational Living*, (No. Hollywood: Wilshire Press, 1998).
65. *Ibid.*, p. 31.
66. *Ibid.*, p. 29.
67. *Ibid.*, p. 26.
68. *Ibid.*, p. 25.
69. *Ibid.*, pp. 111-126.
70. *Enchiridion*, 44.
71. *Ibid.*, 5.
72. Readers interested in the current work of Dr. Ellis are encouraged to visit his web site: www.rebt.org.

Part III: Miscellaneous Matters
1. Seneca, "On Providence," in Hadas, p. 28.
2. Epictetus, *Discourses*, 2.8.14.
3. Marcus Aurelius, *Meditations*, 5.7.
4. *Ibid.*, 6.27.
5. *Discourses*, 4.10.16.
6. William Rowe, *Philosophy of Religion*, (Belmont, CA: Wadsworth, 2001).
7. "On Providence," in Hadas, p. 30.
8. *Meditations*, 5.8.
9. "On Providence," in Hadas, p. 41.
10. *Discourses*, 4.1.10.
11. *Meditations*, 10.3
12. *Discourses*, 1.27.11.
13. *Ibid.*, 1.27
14. *Ibid.*, 2.1.32.
15. *Ibid.*, 4.1.
16. *Dhammapada*, translated by Juan Mascaro (New York: Penguin, 1973), 1.
17. *Ibid.*, 3.
18. *Discourses*, 3.19.3.
19. *Ibid.*, 3.9.2.
20. *Meditations*, 4.7.
21. *Dhammapada*, 1.
22. *Ibid.*, 4.
23. *Meditations*, 4.18.
24. See, for example, Russell, *A History of Western Philosophy*, 228.
25. *Meditations* 4.48.
26. *Dhammapada*, 13.
27. *Meditations*, 4.4.
28. D.T. Suzuki, *An Introduction to Zen Buddhism* (New York: Grove Press, 1964).
29. *Meditations*, 4.16.

Notes

117

30. *Ibid.*, 5.5.
31. *Meditations*, 8.19.
32. *Ibid.*, 4.31.
33. *Ibid.*, 4.44.
34. *Ibid.*, 4.36.
35. *Ibid.*, 11.7.
36. Epictetus, *Discourses*, 3.23.3.
37. *Ibid.*, 1.2.32.
38. *Ibid.*, 3.12.17.
39. *Ibid.*, 4.8.36.
40. *Meditations*, 12.13.
41. Epictetus, *Enchiridion*, 4.
42. *Discourses*, 4.6.34.
43. *Enchiridion*, 21.
44. *Meditations*, 9.37.
45. Seneca, *Letters from a Stoic*, 8.
46. Henry David Thoreau, Walden edited by Joseph Wood Krutch (New York: Bantam, 1968) 269-270.

Index

anger, 36, 56-8
anxiety, 58-60
Aristotle, xiv
Buddhism, 86-90, 90-93
Christian, xii, 22, 41, 81-84
control, xvi, xvii, 19, 37
death, 18-19, 49, 107
depression, 60-61
desire, xv, 87, 99
Ellis, Albert, 69-73
elderly, 23-25
emotions, xix, 53
equilibrium, 14, 50
ethics, xiii-xv
evil , 81-84
eternal goods, xvi, xix, 19, 28
Frankl, Victor, 39
God, 43, 77-80, 82
Goleman, Daniel, 53-54, 56,60,
gratitude, 36, 40, 40, 79, 84
grief, 47-52
happiness, xv, 41, 67-69, 85
health, 26-31
insult, 14-15
joy, xix, 64
Jung, Carl, xiv, 24
love, 15-17
nature, 14, 96
Olympics, xviii, 37
optimism, xx, 62-4, 108
pleasure,95
Plato, xiii
Positive Psychology, 68-69
reason, 58

regret, 38-40
self-awareness, 53-55
self-hatred, 41-44
society, 65-66, 99
Socrates, 78, 98
spirituality, 6
Stoicism, xii-xx, 99-100
suicide, 20-22
tranquility, xviii
travel, 11-12
wealth, 5-7, 9

Printed in Great Britain
by Amazon.co.uk, Ltd.,
Marston Gate.